Biography®

The 14th Dalai LAMA

Whitney Stewart

Lerner Publications Company
Minneapolis

To Tenzin Gyatso and Tenzin Kunga

A&E and **BIOGRAPHY** are trademarks of the A&E Television Networks, registered in the United States and other countries.

Some of the people profiled in this series have also been featured in A&E's acclaimed BIOGRAPHY series, which is available on videocassette from A&E Home Video. Call 1-800-423-1212 to order.

Copyright © 2000 by Whitney Stewart
First published in 1996 by Lerner Publications Company under the title *The 14th Dalai Lama: Spiritual Leader of Tibet*.

First Avenue Editions
A division of Lerner Publishing Group
241 First Avenue North
Minneapolis, MN 55401 U.S.A.

Website address: www.lernerbooks.com

Library of Congress Cataloging-in-Publication Data

Stewart, Whitney, 1959–
   The 14th Dalai Lama / by Whitney Stewart.
     p. cm. — (A&E biography)
   Includes bibliographical references (p.) and index.
   ISBN 0–8225–9691–1 (pbk. : alk. paper)
   1. Bstan-'dzin-rgya-mtsho, Dalai Lama XIV, 1935–   —Juvenile literature.
2. Dalai lamas—Biography—Juvenile literature. 3. Buddhism—China—
Tibet—Juvenile literature. [1. Tenzin Gyatso, Dalai Lama XIV, 1935– . 2.
Dalai lamas.] I. Title. II. Title: Fourteenth Dalai Lama. III. Series.
BQ7935.B777S73 2000
294.3'923'092
[B]   00–010279

Manufactured in the United States of America
1 2 3 4 5 6 – JR – 05 04 03 02 01 00

A C K N O W L E D G M E N T S

In order to complete this book, I received assistance from many people. Good friends took care of my young son in order to give me the time to write. I thank them all for their compassionate care: Christiane Andersson, Liselotte Andersson, Monique Caminade, Marlee Clymer, Megan Clymer, Bernard Pretorius, Anthony Pym, Natalie Stein, Yuli Westenberg, and Miyuki Yamada.

Others gave me moral support and financial aid to travel to Tibet and Dharamsala: I thank Carlin Whitney Scherer, A. George Scherer III, Richard R. Stewart, Cynthia Everets, the late Howard F. Whitney Jr., Dorothy D. Whitney, and Mme. Eleanor Barzin.

Still others have bolstered me, answered questions, or given suggestions: Thanks to Pablo Arias, Naomi S. Baron, Tenzin Choedak, Jeff Cox, Geyche Rinchen Choegyal of Drepung Loseling Monastery, Kenton Clymer, Chung Dolma & Jampa-La, Rinchen Dharlo, Dr. Melvyn Goldstein, Mr. & Mrs. Ted Groll, Khenpo K. Gyaltsen, Heinrich Harrer, Dr. Uwe Hartemann, Lobsang Jinpa, Vickie Lewelling, Ingmar Mounce, Thubten Jigme Norbu, Neema Phentok, Sidney Piburn, Doboom Rinpoche, Lama Samten, Tenzin Sangpo, the Soepa family of McLeod Ganj, Warren Smith, Mr. & Mrs. Phuntsok T. Takla, Mrs. Namgyal L. Samden-Taklha, Tenzin Geyche Tethong, Tehor Kagyur Tulku, Kelsang Wangmo, Thupten Woser, and Mr. & Mrs. Champa Thupten Zongtse.

My friend, Tenzin Taklha, project coordinator of the Tibetan Assistance Project in North America, answered all of my questions with great patience and friendliness. The dedicated Lobsang Yeshi deserves praise for his last-minute research assistance. I thank my editor, Susan Breckner Rose, for her keen eye and sharp editorial cutting instrument. I am grateful to my husband, Hans C. Andersson, and my son, Christoph Andersson, for their cooperation and belief. I have no end of gratitude for His Holiness the Dalai Lama who is my constant inspiration.

—WS

High in the rugged Himalayan Mountains of Tibet, Buddhist monks and nuns live in isolated monasteries.

CONTENTS

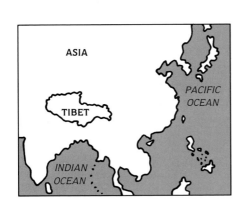

ASIA

PACIFIC
OCEAN

TIBET

INDIAN
OCEAN

TIBET and Surrounding Areas

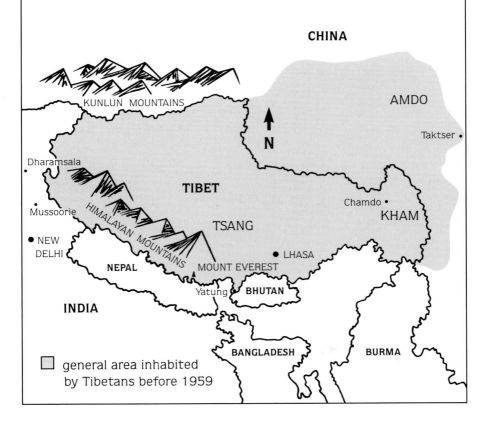

CHINA

KUNLUN MOUNTAINS

AMDO

Taktser •

Dharamsala •

TIBET

N

Chamdo •

Mussoorie •

HIMALAYAN MOUNTAINS

TSANG

KHAM

• NEW
  DELHI

NEPAL

MOUNT EVEREST

• LHASA

Yatung

BHUTAN

INDIA

BANGLADESH

BURMA

general area inhabited
by Tibetans before 1959

INTRODUCTION

THE PLATEAU OF TIBET, HOMELAND OF THE 14TH Dalai Lama, is often called "the Roof of the World" or "the Land of Snows." Located in central Asia and bordered by mountain ranges, the plateau is the largest and highest in the world. In the Himalayan Mountains, which form Tibet's western and southern boundaries, stands Mount Everest—the world's tallest mountain. Its north face looks over Tibetan ridges and rocky soil. Nestled in the sharp ledges below Everest are isolated Tibetan Buddhist monasteries, refuges for Tibetan monks and nuns. Temperatures there often drop as low as −50°F, and powerful winds whip against the rocks. Hail and snowstorms can keep the monks and nuns captive for months. In the highlands of Tibet, nomads graze their yaks and sheep. In the lowlands, Tibetan farmers grow crops including barley—Tibet's main source of nutrition—buckwheat, black peas, and other fruits and vegetables.

Buddhism spread to Tibet from India in the seventh century. The teachings came from Shakyamuni Buddha, who was born as Prince Siddhartha in India in 563 B.C., and who left his life of royalty to uncover a path to the end of suffering. For years he wandered and questioned. He practiced self-denial as a measure of spiritual discipline. He meditated until he gained enlightenment, and he came to be called the "Awakened One," the "Buddha."

Buddha taught that all beings live in a cycle of birth, death, and rebirth. To escape this cycle of continued suffering—called *samsara*—a person must purify his or her body, speech, and mind. The practice of meditation— focusing the mind—is essential. When, after striving to be free of all desires and worldly things, a person quits the cycle, he or she comprehends *nirvana*—complete peace, a state of complete awareness or enlightenment.

Those who actively practice Buddha's teachings aim to become *bodhisattvas,* enlightened beings who choose to reincarnate. In reincarnation, one's deepest level of consciousness moves on to inhabit a new body after death. Bodhisattvas reincarnate lifetime after lifetime to help all other beings out of samsara.

Because understanding the nature of life and having compassion for all beings are the roots of Tibetan Buddhism, many Tibetans try fervently to attain wisdom and achieve altruism. Families at all levels of society send at least one son to a monastery to become a monk so that the entire family can benefit from the son's spiritual development. Some daughters also leave home to live and study in Tibetan Buddhist nunneries. Tibetan Buddhist teachers, or *lamas,* instruct the monastic and the lay communities in Buddhist philosophy. Those lamas who

Tibetan Buddhist monks at their monastery

reincarnate for the benefit of all others are called *tulkus* and are highly respected in Tibetan society. The 14th Dalai Lama is a tulku, and he is revered as a bodhisattva of unconditional compassion.

> We [Tibetans] believed that the Buddha's teaching was the indispensable key to achieving national, as well as individual, happiness. So our whole social system—culture, arts, and lifestyle—was centered on people's spiritual development according to the Dharma [Buddha's teachings].

In disguise, the Dalai Lama and his younger brother Tenzin Choegyal escape from Lhasa.

ESCAPING
TO SAVE
HIS PEOPLE

ON THE NIGHT OF MARCH 17, 1959, AT A FEW minutes before 10:00, the Dalai Lama threw a rifle over his right shoulder to complete his disguise as a foot soldier. Dressed in pants and a long black coat and without his glasses, he passed undetected out of Norbulingka, his summer palace, and through the pressing crowd of his supporters. If the anguished Tibetan people had recognized him, they might have panicked to protect their beloved political and spiritual leader from the Chinese Communist soldiers who had invaded Tibet in 1950.

The Dalai Lama was reluctant to depart from his land and people in the midst of broiling violence between the oppressed Tibetans and the Chinese military forces, but he could find no alternative. "I was convinced that leaving was the only thing I could do to make the crowd disperse. If I was no longer inside, there could be no reason for people to remain."

The 23-year-old Dalai Lama had tried to negotiate calmly with the officers of the Chinese People's Liberation Army, who declared Tibet a part of the "Great Motherland" of China. He had tried to restore peace between his people and the Chinese, but the conflict developed into a hostile crisis.

> FOR THE FIRST TIME IN MY LIFE I WAS TRULY AFRAID — NOT SO MUCH FOR MYSELF BUT FOR THE MILLIONS OF PEOPLE WHO PUT THEIR FAITH IN ME.

Most Tibetans believed that the Chinese were plotting to capture the Dalai Lama and thereby throw the country into turmoil without its Tibetan Buddhist leader. The Dalai Lama's advisers finally convinced him that both he and his country were in great danger.

"The thought of being captured terrified me. For the first time in my life I was truly afraid—not so much for myself but for the millions of people who put their faith in me. If I was caught, all would be lost."

The Dalai Lama and his escape party—including his mother and younger sister and brother, his personal attendants, and many important lamas—had to move swiftly and silently out of Norbulingka, down to the Kyichu River, and across the fast-flowing waters by yak-skin boat. Each splash of the oars threatened to give them away to the thousands of Chinese guards on watch in and around the capital city of Lhasa. The escapees were

The Dalai Lama (wearing dark clothing and glasses), *his guards, and Tibetan freedom fighters rest for a moment on their flight from the Chinese Communists in Lhasa.*

graced with low clouds that shaded the moon and darkened the night.

As soon as they reached the distant riverbank, they met Tibetan freedom fighters who provided ponies. Then the Dalai Lama and his party fled into the mountains. They traveled quickly through the night and into the dawn. At the last mountain pass where he could still see the capital city, the Dalai Lama turned around. Fearful about the fate of his people, he looked sadly down on Lhasa. He prayed for a few minutes and asked himself many questions. Would he see his home again? Would harm come to his people? What could he do now to help Tibet?

Lhamo Thondup as a young child

CHAPTER TWO

BORN IN A COW SHED

ON THE FIFTH DAY OF THE FIFTH MONTH OF THE Wood-Hog Year in the Tibetan calendar—or July 6, 1935— a baby boy was born in a cow shed. He was named Lhamo Thondup, which means "Wish-Fulfilling Goddess."

High in the Amdo region in northeastern Tibet, in the small farming village of Taktser, nobody paid attention to the dark and thundering weather during Lhamo Thondup's birth, nor to the rainbow over the baby's home. Many years later, people said that the rainbow had been a sign of the baby's future importance. Some neighbors did notice a pair of crows on the family's roof, but they did not think twice about the birds then. Now when those neighbors look back, they believe that the crows had come to protect the new baby. Also mysterious was the sudden and unexpected recovery of Choekyong Tsering, the baby's father, who had been critically ill for weeks. Choekyong Tsering believed that his son's birth cured

Faded prayer flags wave in the wind.

him, and he declared his gratitude: "In thanks for my good health, I will make my son a monk."

In front of Lhamo Thondup's home, prayer flags suspended from a tall flagpole cracked in the wind. In their stone and mud house—with a kitchen, an altar room, two bedrooms, a storeroom, and a room for the animals—his family lived in ordinary Tibetan style.

Choekyong Tsering farmed barley, buckwheat, potatoes, and other vegetables. He raised sheep, chickens,

Butter lamps flicker on a Tibetan Buddhist family altar.

goats, and *dzomos*—a cross between a bull and a female yak. With his surplus crops, he bartered for tea, sugar, cotton fabric, and tools. Whenever possible, Choekyong Tsering traded for new horses. A horse lover, he tried to interest Lhamo Thondup in riding, but the boy was always intimidated by the large animals.

Deyki Tsering, Lhamo Thondup's mother, was a cheerful, caring, and deeply compassionate woman. According to Lhamo Thondup, "My mother was undoubtedly one of the kindest people I have ever known. She was truly wonderful and was loved, I am quite certain, by all who knew her."

During a famine in China, poor Chinese people crossed into Tibet in search of food. A Chinese couple came to Deyki Tsering's door carrying a dead child. Deyki Tsering offered to help them bury the child—but they were planning to eat it. Deyki Tsering was so shocked that she gave them all of the food in her cupboards.

In all, Deyki Tsering gave birth to 16 children—Lhamo Thondup was the ninth—but only 7 survived. She also worked in the fields and somehow found time to cook wonderful food. She was known for her breads, which Lhamo Thondup loved to eat with thick cream. She often made *tukpa,* a noodle and meat soup that was her son's favorite dish.

In his earliest years, Lhamo Thondup didn't spend much time with his older siblings. His oldest sister, Tsering Dolma, was 18 years older, and she helped her mother take care of the younger children. She acted as midwife at Lhamo Thondup's birth and was the first to feed the boy an herbal elixir to ensure her new brother's good health.

Lhamo Thondup's eldest brother, Thubten Jigme Norbu, had been recognized as the reincarnation of a Tibetan Buddhist teacher, Taktser Rinpoche, and he was sent to become a monk in the nearby Kumbum Monastery. The second brother, Gyalo Thondup, went away to school in a nearby village. The third brother, Lobsang Samden, was also sent to Kumbum Monastery.

On the occasions when Lhamo Thondup could see Lobsang Samden, they played inseparably and argued unceasingly. Otherwise Lhamo Thondup spent much of his playtime with animals. One of his favorite pastimes was to play in the hens' nest and imitate clucking noises.

He was fearless around most animals and could even pick up a scorpion without flinching.

Life for Lhamo Thondup was nothing unusual for a boy in a Tibetan farming family. When he was old enough to walk, he followed his mother in her household activities. As devoted Buddhists, the family prepared offerings every morning and lit butter lamps on the family altar. After their rituals, they began the farm work of collecting milk, gathering eggs, tending the vegetable garden, and preparing meals. Back then, nobody claimed that Lhamo Thondup was anything but an average toddler.

In retrospect, however, Deyki Tsering thought that some of her son's behavior may have indicated that he knew he was not an ordinary little boy. One of his unusual games was to pretend to pack for a trip. "I'm going to Lhasa. I'm going to Lhasa," Lhamo Thondup would repeat, although nobody had given him the idea of traveling to the capital of Tibet, thousands of miles away. Lhamo Thondup also insisted that he sit at the head of the dining table and that nobody but his mother touch his food bowl. This could indicate that the boy had a strong character, or, on the other hand, that he knew he was a person of great importance. He also had several dreams that could be interpreted as signs; but later, even he could not be sure of the significance of the dreams. "I cannot say categorically that I knew of my future all along," he admitted. Whether or not Lhamo Thondup was aware of his destiny does not change the fact that, by the time he was three years old, his life would change drastically.

Chenrezig, the deity of perfect compassion. Tibetan Buddhists believe the Dalai Lama is the human incarnation of Chenrezig and the embodiment of compassion.

THE CONTINUING CONSCIOUSNESS

IN 1933 THE RELIGIOUS AND POLITICAL LEADER OF Tibet—the 13th Dalai Lama, Thupten Gyatso—died, and the ministers of Tibet busied themselves with plans to find their leader's reincarnation. The Dalai Lama is believed to be reincarnated. In other words, his consciousness does not die with his body but moves on to inhabit a new body.

Tibetan Buddhists believe that the Dalai Lama is the human incarnation of *Chenrezig,* the deity of compassion. Chenrezig reincarnates to help all beings find their way out of the suffering of life. Tibetans revere the Dalai Lama, not just as a political leader, but also as an enlightened protector. Whenever Tibetans see the Dalai Lama, they bow or prostrate themselves on the ground in front of their leader to show respect. When the Dalai Lama dies, the entire country is anxious to find the reincarnation as quickly as possible.

The title of "Dalai Lama" was first used in the 1500s, more than 100 years after Tsong Khapa founded the Gelukpa sect of Tibetan Buddhism. Three other sects of Tibetan Buddhism had already been formed: the Kagyu, the Nyingma, and the Sakya. The Gelukpa sect became the fourth and largest. The sects have different practices and prayers, but they were all founded on the teachings of Buddha, called the dharma.

The third Gelukpa lama, Sonam Gyatso, was invited to Mongolia in 1578 by Altan Khan, the ruler, to teach the Mongols about the way of the Buddha. Altan Khan was so inspired by Sonam Gyatso's teaching that he declared Buddhism as law in Mongolia. He also gave Sonam Gyatso the formal title "Dalai Lama," which is loosely translated as "Ocean of Wisdom."

In the late 1500s, during the life of the fourth Dalai Lama, Tibet was troubled by conflicts between different religious sects and by envy among minor kings. The Gelukpa sect was gaining power in Tibet, and it maintained close ties with the Mongols. By the 1600s, when the fifth Dalai Lama reached maturity, a Mongol prince, Gushri Khan, had invaded Tibet and fought off all opponents of the Gelukpa sect. Gushri Khan then declared himself king of Tibet, and he assigned control of the country to the fifth Dalai Lama.

The fifth Dalai Lama, often called the "Great Fifth,"

was the strongest ruler Tibet had ever known. He organized a federal government and divided power between religious and secular authorities throughout Tibet. The Great Fifth moved his seat of power from Drepung Monastery to Lhasa, where he had the great Potala Palace built on the site of a former king's fortress. When the

The 1,000-room Potala Palace, built by the fifth Dalai Lama, overlooks Lhasa.

The fifth Dalai Lama, the "Great Fifth"

Great Fifth died in 1682, his attendants did not want the public to know of the death until the Potala Palace was finished. For the next 15 years, the attendants declared that the Great Fifth was in a long retreat. A regent governed Tibet until the secret was exposed in 1697. The sixth Dalai Lama, born in 1683, was then enthroned. Unlike his predecessor, the sixth Dalai Lama spent more time drinking *chang* (Tibetan rice beer), courting women, and writing poetry than he did studying Tibetan Buddhism. He was declared a false incarnation by the Mongol chieftain and sent into exile. He disappeared in the Koko Nor region of Tibet on his way to China.

The next six reincarnations were not strong. The young dalai lamas died in their youth, were murdered, or were controlled by ministers who fought among themselves for power in Lhasa. Even so, the dalai lamas maintained Tibet's relations with the Mongol warlords and later the Manchu emperors in China. These arrangements were based on interdependence between countries—Tibet offered spiritual protection to China, while the Mongol, and later the Manchu leaders, offered military protection to Tibet. During periods of unrest in Tibet and in China, the Chinese did try to influence the Tibetan government. China kept soldiers and two officials in Tibet, but these people did not control the country.

The 13th Dalai Lama changed the course of his country. He strengthened the Tibetan government, began to build an army, and sent children abroad to have a Western education. He examined his political system, which

was administered by lay officials selected from aristocratic families and by monk officials who came from the
middle class. Wherever he found inefficiency, the 13th
Dalai Lama tried to reorganize. He wanted to reduce the
influence of the great monasteries upon the government.

By bringing in an electric generator and a few cars, the
13th Dalai Lama introduced Western technology to Tibet.

The 13th Dalai Lama

He knew that if his country did not end its isolation from the rest of the world, it would be in danger. He warned:

> It may happen that here in Tibet, religion and government will be attacked both from without and within. Unless we guard our own country, it will now happen that the Dalai [Lama] . . . and all the revered holders of the Faith will disappear and become nameless. Monks and their monasteries will be destroyed. The rule of law will be weakened. The lands and properties of government officials will be seized. They themselves will be forced to serve their enemies or wander the country like beggars. All beings will be sunk in great hardship and overwhelming fear; the days and nights will drag on slowly in suffering.

With the fall of the Manchu dynasty during the Chinese revolution in 1911, Tibet's relations with China broke down. The 13th Dalai Lama discussed this breakdown with his British friend, Sir Charles Bell:

> The connection with China was the connection between the Dalai Lama and the Manchu Emperor. The Manchus were considered as Buddhists; the Chinese were not. When the Chinese revolution broke out in 1911, China deposed the Manchu Emperor. There was then no longer that connection between the two. Tibet is now completely separate from China.

After the collapse of relations between the Tibetans and the Manchus, the 13th Dalai Lama expelled all Chinese soldiers and civilians from Tibet and made a formal declaration of independence. He broke all ties with China that might be misunderstood by the new Chinese government and reclaimed Tibet as a fully independent country.

When the 13th Dalai Lama died in Lhasa, on December 17, 1933, singing and dancing were banned and people wore dark clothing to mourn the loss of their great

TIBET IS NOW COMPLETELY SEPARATE FROM CHINA.

leader. Political intrigue and argument stirred up over the selection of the regent, the temporary leader, who would serve as political ruler until the 14th Dalai Lama was found and grew old enough to lead Tibet himself.

One of the 13th Dalai Lama's trusted attendants, Kumbela, was in a good position to take power as regent. Many members of the *kashag,* the Tibetan government's cabinet, were in favor of bringing Kumbela to power.

Several other officials were secretly trying to lead their own campaigns to eliminate Kumbela and rise to power themselves. Some of these men tried to gain favor with the powerful Sera, Drepung, and Ganden Monasteries, and others used their influence with the military. One campaign implicated Kumbela in the sudden death of the 13th Dalai Lama, making Kumbela look like an assassin. Another campaign influenced soldiers under Kumbela's power to mutiny, leaving Kumbela without military strength. These rivals of Kumbela proved to be too strong, and eventually Kumbela and his allies were sentenced to exile from Lhasa. Kumbela was formally charged with the crime of not having reported the 13th Dalai Lama's illness to the government before the leader's death.

After the Kumbela scandal, the kashag decided that an incarnate lama should be chosen as regent, so that the people would have a temporary spiritual leader as well as a temporary political leader. After a great amount of disagreement and deliberation, a former abbot of Ganden Monastery carried out a divination. After stabilizing his mind in a deep, meditative state, he cast a die two times. Then he interpreted the letters that came up on the die. He recommended that Reting Rinpoche, a 24-year-old incarnate lama, be chosen.

Even with Reting Rinpoche as head of state, the political complications in the country did not cease. The monasteries—which had many representatives in the government—were against the 13th Dalai Lama's modernization programs. The lay officials who supported modernization did not want to accept leadership that sided with the monastic officials. Some officials continued to tangle themselves in a web of political power. Others turned their attention to the search for the 14th Dalai Lama, who they believed had been reborn somewhere in Tibet.

Lamas searched the four corners of Tibet for the 14th incarnation of the Dalai Lama.

THE AUSPICIOUS DISCOVERY

FINDING THE 14TH DALAI LAMA WAS NO SIMPLE task. Lamas in Lhasa had to carry out a procedure for discovery that was steeped in tradition, and they had to outwit those who hoped to foil their efforts.

The lamas who were charged with finding the next Dalai Lama had a few clues with which to begin their hunt. When the body of the 13th Dalai Lama was placed in the lotus position on his tomb in Norbulingka, his face looked toward the south. Monks attending to the body said that later the Dalai Lama faced east. They believed that this change indicated something important about the eastern region of Tibet.

After the 13th Dalai Lama's death, elephants of different sizes appeared in cloud formations in the northeastern part of the sky—another sign about eastern Tibet. And finally, the monks noticed that when the golden *chorten,* or temple, was built to entomb the late 13th Dalai Lama, a star-shaped fungus grew on a wooden column on the northeastern side of the construction. "These many signs made everyone feel sure that the Dalai Lama would be reincarnated in the east of Tibet," wrote a member of the search party. So the regent sent his searchers to the northeast, to the Amdo region of Tibet.

Reting Rinpoche, the regent, wanted to be very thorough in his search for the next Dalai Lama. He believed that the waters of Lake Lhamoi Lhatso could reveal sacred visions to the faithful. So in 1935, the *rinpoche* took the 10-day journey southeast of Lhasa to the sacred lake in hopes of obtaining more clues about the new incarnation. For many days, he prayed and meditated at the edge of the lake until he had a vision. He saw three Tibetan letters: *Ah, Ka, Ma.* Then he had a vision of a monastery with a turquoise and golden roof. Finally he saw a small house with strange gutters that stood behind an old poplar tree.

On September 5, 1936—the Tibetan Fire-Rat Year—Kyitsang Rinpoche, an important lama from Sera Monastery, prepared for a long search. With no paved roads in Tibet at that time, travelers did their best going over rocky mountain passes and through clouds of dust. Other monks were sent out to the Chamdo and Dokham areas of Tibet, but Kyitsang Rinpoche and three attendants were sent to Amdo. The night before the men departed, a heavy snowfall left deep snowbanks along the trail. At 9:00 the next morning, the party gathered together. Suddenly the sky became clear and the sun melted the snow. "This sudden change in weather caused great astonishment to our party."

Now that the trails were clear, the group could start on its way. They began an expedition that took months of trudging through the snow, climbing over mountains, and walking across endless meadows. The men pushed on and on, even traveling at night in order to make progress through the aggressive weather.

After more than three months of travel, the party arrived at the Kumbum Monastery in Amdo. As soon as they saw the monastery, the men realized that it was the monastery reflected in the sacred waters of Lhamoi Lhatso. The turquoise roof was unmistakable. Then they also understood the meaning of the letters that Reting Rinpoche had seen. *Ah* probably stood for the Amdo region of Tibet, and *Ka* for Kumbum Monastery. *Ka* and *Ma* were also thought to indicate the Karma Sharston Hermitage, an important place of worship in the Amdo region.

Now the monks needed to find the house with the strange gutters and the big poplar tree. This last task, however, would not be easy. Because many political factions were trying to take control of Tibet, the search party led by Kyitsang Rinpoche operated with great diplomacy and discretion. The search party was preoccupied with the safety of the 14th Dalai Lama.

Before Kyitsang Rinpoche could go in search of candidates for the reincarnation, he had to meet with Ma Pu-Feng, the local Chinese governor—a Muslim warlord who in the 1930s had aggressively established a government in Amdo that was part of the Chinese Republic. To carry out their search, the lamas had to obtain permission from Ma Pu-Feng. Tibetan officials in the area recommended that Kyitsang Rinpoche and his party bring special gifts in order to show respect to the Chinese governor. The lamas gathered together gold, silver, incense, and silk wool, which they offered to Ma Pu-Feng, who responded with formal courtesy. As soon as homage was paid, the men were allowed to proceed with their search.

Of all the possible candidates, Kyitsang Rinpoche would visit three. One of the boys died before the rinpoche could reach him. Of the remaining two, one was very shy and showed no inclination to greet the rinpoche. The third child, however, displayed some promising signs. Lhamo Thondup was that child.

Kyitsang Rinpoche disguised himself as a servant in a sheepskin cloak on his visit to Lhamo Thondup's home—a house covered with gutters made of juniper wood, standing next to a poplar tree. One of his attendants pretended to be the honored leader of the party. When the men arrived at the door, the honored leader was invited into the front rooms of the home, while the disguised Kyitsang Rinpoche entered the family's living quarters. In this way, the rinpoche unceremoniously observed the little boy named Lhamo Thondup.

During the monks' visit, Lhamo Thondup became quite friendly with Kyitsang Rinpoche and climbed up onto the lama's lap. In order to examine the boy's reaction to items that had belonged to the 13th Dalai Lama, Kyitsang Rinpoche wrapped the 13th Dalai Lama's rosary around

Lhamo Thondup looks like a typical peasant boy.

his own neck. Before long, Lhamo Thondup reached out and touched the rosary and asked for it.

"You may have it if you can say who I am," responded Kyitsang Rinpoche.

"Sera Lama," exclaimed Lhamo Thondup indicating that he knew Kyitsang Rinpoche was a lama from Sera Monastery in Lhasa.

The boy then went on to identify the other monks in the room who were also from Sera. The curious point is that Lhamo Thondup had never been formally introduced to the monks, and he had never, in his present lifetime, been to Lhasa, the capital of Tibet.

Maintaining calm and keeping their hopes to themselves, Kyitsang Rinpoche and his attendants spent the night at Lhamo Thondup's house. Again and again, Lhamo Thondup climbed up onto the rinpoche's lap and stared at the rosary. The next morning, when it became time for the lamas to depart, Lhamo Thondup began to cry and begged to be taken along. "This made it very hard for the search party to take leave of the child," wrote a member of Kyitsang Rinpoche's party.

Although the search party had high hopes for its latest candidate, the lamas had to ask permission from the Tibetan government in Lhasa to examine each candidate. After four weeks, the search party received a message from Lhasa.

Carrying many articles that had belonged to the 13th Dalai Lama—a yellow rosary, a black rosary, a walking stick, and an ivory drum bejeweled in turquoise—the men set out to see Lhamo Thondup again. The monks heard a conch shell being blown as they departed, which they interpreted as a sign of good fortune. Along the way, the men stopped at a fork in the road, and there a young Chinese man advised them to take the lower road. Along that road, the monks came upon a sacred place where the 13th Dalai Lama had rested during one of his many pilgrimages. Supposedly the 13th Dalai Lama had once spotted the house where Lhamo Thondup would be born and had commented on its beauty. When the monks arrived at Lhamo Thondup's home, they realized that the lower road they had taken was longer than the higher road, but it led directly to the front door of the house. Because of this, the lamas wondered if the Chinese man could have been a celestial being who came to show the way to Lhamo Thondup's house. When Lhamo Thondup's mother saw the lamas on her doorstep, she invited them in for tea and fresh, Amdo-style bread.

After tea, Kyitsang Rinpoche asked Lhamo Thondup's parents for permission to question the young boy. Kyitsang Rinpoche laid out the objects belonging to the 13th Dalai Lama next to similar objects that were never used by the late Dalai Lama. Kyitsang Rinpoche then asked Lhamo Thondup to choose the articles that he preferred. He chose the correct rosary, and this caused a great stir among the monks.

When it came time for Lhamo Thondup to choose the correct walking stick, however, the monks felt momentary panic. Lhamo Thondup first pulled at the incorrect walking stick and held it for a moment. The monks watched anxiously. Suddenly he dropped that stick, picked up the correct one, and grasped it firmly. Later the monks found out that both walking sticks had belonged to the 13th Dalai Lama, but the first one had been given away to another lama.

With one more test to be made, the rinpoche held out two hand drums. Again the monks watched the boy with apprehension. The incorrect drum was beautifully decorated with colored silk and floral patterns. But Lhamo Thondup chose the correct drum without hesitation.

The monks had found the next Dalai Lama!

> Now that we had witnessed these miraculous performances, our minds were filled with deep devotion, joy, and gaiety. Indeed we were so moved that tears of happiness filled our eyes; scarcely able to breathe, we could neither sit properly on the mat or speak a word. Then, unable to think what to do next, we just sat gazing fondly at each other, praying no obstacles would arise.

That night, the lamas stayed again at Lhamo Thondup's house and talked to the boy's parents. Kyitsang Rinpoche did not reveal the discovery even to them. Instead, he asked them if they had seen any signs of the child's importance.

"No, there was nothing of that sort," responded Choekyong Tsering and Deyki Tsering.

The neighbors, however, did point out events that could be interpreted as signs of good fortune. They remembered that Choekyong Tsering had been miserably ill until the birth of his son. They also remembered the splendid rainbow that had seemed to touch the boy's house when he was born. With all that the monks had seen and heard, they believed there was no mistake. Before they could make any grand declarations, however, the monks had to send a coded message to Lhasa describing their discovery and requesting a plan for taking Lhamo Thondup to Lhasa. They did not want to leak the secret to the Chinese government, which was looking for a way to control Tibetan politics.

After several days, Kyitsang Rinpoche received an answer from Lhasa. Tibetan officials in Lhasa considered all of the information from Kyitsang Rinpoche's search. This information concurred with what the regent had seen in his visions at Lake Lhamoi Lhatso. The boy's behavior also convinced officials of his identity. Now the Tibetans had to devise a plan to bring Lhamo Thondup, the 14th Dalai Lama, to the capital city. They were afraid that the Chinese governor, Ma Pu-Feng, would use this discovery to increase his own power.

While Kyitsang Rinpoche arranged travel plans, which took nearly two years, the Dalai Lama was taken by his parents to Kumbum Monastery. There his older brothers were already installed as reincarnated lamas. The boy did not want to be left without his parents. He cried when he saw his mother depart. His brothers had to tell Lhamo Thondup that Deyki Tsering had just gone out for watermelon and would return soon. When Choekyong Tsering

An attendant carries the new Dalai Lama across the courtyard of Kumbum Monastery.

left, the young Dalai Lama was anguished, feeling alone in unfamiliar surroundings. His only comforts were that his brother Lobsang Samden was there and that he had a gentle old monk as a teacher. Otherwise, the three-year-old boy felt lonely and abandoned, and he did not understand the change in his life.

Ma Pu-Feng did find out that Lhamo Thondup was the likely candidate for the reincarnation, and he demanded an enormous sum of money from the Tibetans. For 18 months, he prevented the Tibetans from departing for Lhasa. And then, as soon as they were able to pay him, he tried to demand even more money for the release of the young Dalai Lama from his province. Not until the summer of 1939—the Tibetan Earth-Hare Year—when the Dalai Lama was four years old, were the Tibetans able to start on their way to Lhasa. "When eventually the great day dawned, a week after my fourth birthday," wrote the Dalai Lama, "I remember a tremendous feeling of optimism."

The large escort party of about 50 people included his parents, nine-year-old Gyalo Thondup, six-year-old Lobsang Samden, government officials, the search party, Muslim traders who had lent the money to pay off Ma

The Dalai Lama's escort party prepares to depart from Kumbum Monastery for a two-month journey across the Himalaya to Lhasa.

Pu-Feng, several religious pilgrims, and 350 horses and mules. They readied themselves for three months of hard travel. Lhamo Thondup and Lobsang Samden were put together in one *dreljam,* a type of enclosed chair carried by two mules, and their mother was in another. The others rode on horseback or walked. The landscape was arid and endless, offering little comfort to the travelers. They crossed frigid mountain passes, wide plains, and frozen streams. They passed small villages every few days, and they spotted remote monasteries high up on rocky ledges. Occasionally the boredom of constant motion became too great for Lhamo Thondup, and he began to fight with Lobsang Samden. Then the *dreljam* driver had to stop the mules and call the boys' mother to settle things. The Dalai Lama wrote:

> When she looked inside, she always found the same thing: Lobsang Samden in tears and me sitting there with a look of triumph on my face. For despite his greater age, I was the more forthright. . . . Lobsang Samden was too good-natured that he could not bring himself to use his superior strength against me.

Deyki Tsering treated the boys to some sweet dried fruit, and this took their attention from fighting.

As soon as the party was beyond the region controlled by Ma Pu-Feng, the Tibetan government formally declared Lhamo Thondup the 14th Dalai Lama. When the travelers finally reached the outskirts of Lhasa in the autumn of 1939, a group of officials was waiting to greet them. There, on the Doeguthang Plain, stood a camp with a large blue-and-white tent shielding a hand-carved wooden throne. The throne was used to honor the new incarnation of the Dalai Lama and to welcome him home. The officials then carried out a special, all-day ceremony during which the 14th Dalai Lama was granted the title of religious leader of the Tibetan people.

When the time came for the new Dalai Lama and his family to enter Lhasa, the escort party took them directly to Norbulingka, the summer palace of the dalai lamas.

Norbulingka, the dalai lamas' summer palace

The new Dalai Lama is seated on the Lion Throne in the Potala Palace. The swastikas, woven into the tapestry, are ancient symbols of good-luck in Tibet and other parts of Asia.

CHAPTER FIVE

ENCLOSED IN A PALACE

THE NEW DALAI LAMA WAS GIVEN SPECIAL apartments at Norbulingka. His parents and brothers moved to a comfortable house on the palace grounds. Although he would soon begin the rigorous education and training reserved for young dalai lamas, at Norbulingka he was allowed some freedom. Having no special obligations yet, he played with Lobsang Samden, walked in the gardens, and talked to the many animals that had been brought to the summer palace—tame musk deer, Tibetan mastiff dogs, mountain goats, a monkey, two-humped Mongolian camels, parrots, peacocks, Canada geese, cranes, and two leopards and a tiger in cages.

Lhamo Thondup liked to sneak off to his parents' new house to find good things to eat. He begged his parents for eggs or pork, which were normally forbidden to him. These foods were believed to inhibit his emerging intelligence. Defying his dietary restrictions, the Dalai Lama often sat next to his father with a wistful, hungry look until his father handed him some pork crackle. Once, an attendant caught the Dalai Lama eating eggs. Instead of hiding the food or running away, the young boy shouted "Get out!" He was already a willful ruler.

In the winter of 1940, the Dalai Lama was taken from Norbulingka to the austere Potala Palace. There he would be ceremoniously enthroned upon the bejeweled Lion Throne, located in the main hall in the east wing of the palace. This noble seat, placed upon eight carved and painted snow lions, was the symbol of political and spiritual leadership in Tibet. The mythical snow lion, with its huge, wild eyes and green mane and tail, heralds Tibetan Buddhism.

On February 22, 1940, when he was not quite five years old, the Dalai Lama became the undisputed spiritual head of Tibet in an elaborate ritual:

> The ceremonies were interminable. There were long, sonorous invocations, interspersed with the bass roar of the four-yard-long *dung-chen* or "great horn"; the trilling and ringing of the *drilbu* or hand-bell; the cry, like an English hunting horn, of the *gyalings;* and the beating of many kinds of drums, from the rigid patter of the little hand-held *damaru* to the deep, dull, unearthly thump of drums that took two monks to carry. There were little ceremonial dances with music and mime, and debates on Buddhist topics. . . . All through this, the little boy sat with perfect composure, dispensing blessings in the appropriate way to

the hundreds of people who came to pay homage, although no one had shown him how.

Shortly after the ceremony, the Dalai Lama was escorted to the Jokhang Temple in the center of Lhasa and inducted into monastic life. During another elaborate ritual, his hair was shaved off by his teacher, and he was dressed in the maroon robes of a monk. Following tradition, he formally gave up his name, Lhamo Thondup, and took on his proper spiritual names. His full name became Jamphel Ngawang Lobsang Yeshe Tenzin Gyatso. In the Western world, he is most commonly called either His Holiness the Dalai Lama or simply Tenzin Gyatso. By Tibetans, he is called Gyalwa Rinpoche, Yeshi Norbu, or Kundun.

ALL THROUGH THIS, THE LITTLE BOY SAT WITH PERFECT COMPOSURE, DISPENSING BLESSINGS IN THE APPROPRIATE WAY TO THE HUNDREDS OF PEOPLE WHO CAME TO PAY HOMAGE, ALTHOUGH NO ONE HAD SHOWN HIM HOW.

The Dalai Lama and Lobsang Samden moved into the Potala, and their family was granted aristocratic status and given a house below the Potala. The Dalai Lama had to follow a restricted routine inside dark confines. "The Potala was not a nice place to live," he wrote.

This great edifice, constructed on a rocky hill during the 1600s, was built from huge slabs of stone, without nails or cement. More than just a palace, it was the burial place of the former dalai lamas and a center for government offices and storerooms. The Potala also housed Namgyal Monastery, home to 175 monks. Dark spiral

The Potala Palace

staircases led to more than 1,000 rooms and 10,000 altars aglow with golden statues and butter lamps. Heavy smoke from incense clung to thick curtains and woolen rugs in the living quarters.

In his bedroom, which once belonged to the fifth Dalai Lama, the boy quivered with fear. He was afraid of the dark. He wondered what could be hidden in the cold, gloomy corners or in the thick dust that had collected behind the drapery on each wall. Night after night, he listened to mice running across the room to eat the food offerings on the altar. Hearing the mice crunching on food made him feel a little less lonely.

Almost a year after the Dalai Lama arrived in Lhasa, his sister Tsering Dolma and his brother Taktser Rinpoche were reunited with their family in Lhasa. The Dalai Lama was allowed to visit them all from time to time. His mother gave birth to another daughter, Jetsun Pema, and later to another son, Tenzin Choegyal. Every month or so, some of his family members would visit the Dalai Lama in the Potala.

For three years, the Dalai Lama shared the palace with Lobsang Samden. During the day, the Potala was not as frightening as during the night. Together the brothers explored the long hallways and abandoned storerooms. They often ran off and hid to see how long they could remain undiscovered. While creeping around from dark room to dark room, they found a large collection of toys and gadgets. Some of the objects had belonged to the 13th Dalai Lama, and others had been sent by foreign dignitaries to the 14th Dalai Lama. Day after day, the two boys delighted in their new playground until several monk officials stopped the fun. The officials did not approve of the boys' games, so they decided to send Lobsang Samden away to school.

Having lost his best friend, the eight-year-old Dalai Lama had to entertain himself with whatever he could find. He took apart and rebuilt old music boxes and watches, he ran his favorite clockwork train set, and he staged wars with a collection of toy soldiers. He lined up the soldiers in beautiful formation and then watched them fall when his battles began.

Sometimes he begged his attendants to play with him. They competed in making model tanks and airplanes out of fresh barley dough. Each player was given the same amount of dough to build an army. The Dalai Lama was good with his hands, so he often won at this stage of the contest. When the armies were ready, the players started the battle. At this point, the monks played enthusiastically, and they did not make the game easy for their young leader. The Dalai Lama often flew into a rage if he lost. "I played very forcefully. Quite often I lost my temper and used my fists, but they still did not give in. Sometimes they even made me cry."

One of the Dalai Lama's favorite pastimes was to observe city life through his telescope. At the base of the hill below the Potala was a prison, and he spent hours watching the prisoners. He considered them friends. When the prisoners noticed him above, they often fell to their knees to show respect to their beloved leader.

The Dalai Lama also watched the busy outdoor life of Lhasa. In the streets below, the peasants and nobles bartered for food and goods, gathered in the streets to chat, or walked—deep in prayer—around temples. Dressed in their finest silks and heavy turquoise jewelry, wealthy Tibetans celebrated holy days, rode horses

Traders from all over Tibet converge on the main market street of Lhasa to sell their wares and gather news.

through the streets, and visited friends. The poorer people were no less interested in festive celebrations, good food, and watching street entertainers. Although the Dalai Lama could not take part in this ordinary life, he shared some of the fun through his telescope, and he developed a deep affection for his people.

Less pleasant for the Dalai Lama was to witness herders bringing their yaks to be slaughtered. Although Tibetan Buddhism does not prohibit meat eating—and the Dalai Lama enjoyed eating meat—Buddhist texts say that animals should not be killed for food. Tibetan monks vow not to kill any conscious being. The Dalai Lama grieved for the animals and requested to buy as many of them as possible. In this way he saved more than 10,000 animals from the butcher.

The hardest part of his day came at sunset when he heard young children coming home from a day of grazing yaks. As the children trotted down the streets singing songs, the young Dalai Lama often felt sorry for himself, shut away in his lonely palace. He had no choice but to live by the rules set for his position. The Dalai Lama was always secluded so that he lived free of ordinary distractions and negative influences. With few worries, he could focus on spiritual development. He was surrounded by brilliant Buddhist scholars and faithful attendants who helped him focus on generating positive spiritual and mental strength.

Although the Dalai Lama felt isolated without his family or playmates his age, he was never really alone. Three monks were assigned to look after him, and they became his constant companions. The *Simpon Khenpo* took care of his clothing, the *Solpon Khenpo* prepared his food, and the *Chopon Khenpo* was in charge of his daily rituals. The boy became especially close to the Solpon Khenpo.

> When I was very young I developed a close attach-
> ment to the Master of the Kitchen. So strong was it
> that he had to be in my sight at all times, even if it
> was only the bottom of his robe visible through a
> doorway or under the curtains which served as
> doors inside Tibetan houses. . . . I sometimes think
> the act of bringing food is one of the basic roots of
> all relationships.

From dawn until dusk, the Dalai Lama was surrounded by attendants, guards, teachers, and government officials; his life was a constant routine. Every morning, he got up at 6:00 and was helped to dress before spending an hour praying and meditating.

The Dalai Lama learned to meditate as a way to train his mind. He learned that Buddhist philosophy is practiced using the body, speech, and mind. Of these three levels of expression, the mind is most important. He later wrote: "One needs to tame the mind. One needs a strong mind, a concentrated mind. Therefore, one needs to develop calm abiding." Through meditation, the Dalai Lama discovered how to calm the wild thoughts, or consciousness, that cluttered his mind. When his mind became trained, then he could grasp the true nature of phenomena and focus on ways to benefit all beings. He would develop great compassion.

After meditation, his first meal of the day was served. He ate a typical Tibetan breakfast of butter tea and *tsampa* with honey or caramel. Tsampa—roasted barley meal—is the mainstay of the Tibetan diet. Tibetans consume endless amounts of tea, usually black tea with butter brewed into it.

When he finished breakfast, the Dalai Lama moved to the veranda next to his bedroom and started his first study period of the day. He had to learn to read and write. The Tibetan language has two main writing systems—one for manuscripts and the other for personal and business letters—and the Dalai Lama had to learn both.

Next the Dalai Lama had lessons in memorizing Buddhist scriptures. He had to memorize text after text to recite to his teacher later in the day. He memorized quickly, so the class was very boring. "I should say, though, that I often forgot just as quickly," he admitted.

After memorization class, the Dalai Lama had to attend a daily government meeting. He was formally escorted from his room to the meeting hall, where he was greeted by all the governmental officials. Although he did not have any political responsibilities yet, he was being groomed for the political position that he would take on when he was older.

The Dalai Lama had still more classes after the meeting. He was obliged to sit with Ling Rinpoche—his junior tutor from the time the Dalai Lama was 6 until he was 15—and recite the text he had memorized earlier in the day. Before the end of this period, Ling Rinpoche explained a new text and required the boy to learn it. Day after day, text after text, the Dalai Lama went on

Ling Rinpoche, who later became the Dalai Lama's senior tutor, and Trijang Rinpoche, the junior tutor

memorizing and learning the many Buddhist scriptures that would give him a deep foundation in Buddhist theory. The scriptures set forth the teachings of the Buddha, which explain ethics, how to meditate, and how to attain wisdom—discriminating between the positive and negative aspects of one's internal and external life.

All of this work lasted until noon, when the conch was blown at the palace. The boy was then free to play until his 1:00 P.M. lunch of soup and bread. After lunch, the sun passed his windows, and his room became dark and cold. This made the Dalai Lama sad and bored, and he was in no mood to continue studying. "I was a very reluctant pupil and disliked all subjects equally," wrote the Dalai Lama.

His afternoon courses consisted of typical subjects for all Tibetan Buddhist monks. As he grew older, he studied Tibetan art, culture, and poetry, but he focused mainly on Buddhist philosophy, logic, and debating. Tibetan monks spend a great deal of their study time in debate; they take turns asking each other difficult logic questions and trying to stump their classmates. The debates can be quite entertaining because of the bold hand gestures that are part of the art of debating. When the debates become funny, the monks laugh heartily at each other.

After working all afternoon with his tutors and taking tea at 4:00 P.M., the Dalai Lama returned to his telescope or played games inside until his dinner was served at about 7:00 P.M. This meal usually consisted of a soup called *tukpa* or ground meat in dumplings called *momos,* some yogurt, and a great deal of homemade bread that his mother brought with her on her visits to the Potala. He often ate with his attendants, monks from Namgyal monastery. He enjoyed their company, especially when the conversation was lively. After dinner the Dalai Lama was supposed to go down into his courtyard to say his recitations and prayers, but when he was very young he did not often do as he was told. Instead he made up his own stories before going to bed at 9:00 P.M.

The Dalai Lama's routine and studies prepared him well for his role as a Tibetan Buddhist leader and teacher, but they did not provide him with much understanding

As a child, the Dalai Lama spent much of his time studying.

of world politics and international relations. His teachers tried to discourage his interest in worldly affairs, but even as a young boy, the Dalai Lama was very curious about life beyond the palace. His great difficulty was finding a way to learn all that he wanted to know.

As a teenager, the Dalai Lama learned more about the lives of typical Tibetans and about the world outside of Tibet.

CONTACT WITH THE WORLD

As THE DALAI LAMA GREW UP, HE CAME INTO more contact with the outside world. He found that he preferred the company of the lively palace servants to that of the serious government and monastic officials. From the servants, he learned about social injustice in his country.

The Tibetan people were bonded together by their Buddhist religion and their love of the Dalai Lama, but they still lived in a feudal society. Almost half of the population lived a nomadic life. More than half of the land belonged to the great monasteries or to the noble class. Peasants, or serfs, rarely had their own land. They were allowed to farm one quarter to one half of the monastic or manorial estates. Manorial estates were passed down in a noble family. Nobles paid no wages to their peasant laborers and allowed them no education. The serfs were required to harvest the noble's crop, fix his house, collect his firewood, and transport his crops and goods.

Serfdom was the foundation for the manorial estate system and for the political and monastic system. It was an efficient system of economic exploitation that guaranteed to the country's religious and secular elites a permanent and secure labor force to cultivate their landholdings without burdening them either with any direct day-to-day responsibility for the serf's subsistence or with the need to compete for labor in a market context.

The Dalai Lama's servants told him how Tibet's wealthy landowners and high lamas often mistreated the servants. Monastic officials, wanting to retain their

A typical peasant plows a field with the help of his yaks.

In the courtyard of a monastery, monks gesture as they practice the ancient art of debate.

power, continually plotted to block modernizations that could change the traditional feudal system. They put down efforts to build up social systems, to create a strong military defense, to educate the people, or to initiate international relations.

The 14th Dalai Lama felt compassion for the poor and weak people in his country, and he wanted to bring about changes in the land ownership system, but he was still too young to wield enough power to change his country.

He wrote: "By nature I have always had a feeling of close-ness with the poor, the helpless and the weak. . . . not only for human beings, but for animals, too."

For the time being, however, he could do very little to modernize Tibetan society. He knew little about ordinary life in Tibet and even less about life in other countries—and he had few people to teach him about the world. He spent hours looking through many illustrated history and geography books and popular magazines that he had found among the 13th Dalai Lama's belongings. He tried to study English with one of his officials, and when Lobsang Samden visited each month, the Dalai Lama fervently questioned his brother for details of daily life in Lhasa.

> BY NATURE I HAVE ALWAYS HAD A FEELING OF CLOSENESS WITH THE POOR, THE HELPLESS AND THE WEAK.

In 1949 the Dalai Lama learned about two Austrians who had arrived in Lhasa. At the time, fewer than 10 Westerners lived in Tibet. Heinrich Harrer and Peter Aufschnaiter had been prisoners of the British in India during World War II. The two escaped their prison camp, crossed India, and made their way on foot through the Himalaya into Tibet. After about five years of nomadic traveling over rocky passes and through snow, ice, and freezing wind, the two Austrians reached Lhasa and somehow avoided being thrown out. Tibet's government was very strict about the visits of foreigners. Harrer and Aufschnaiter learned to speak Tibetan and made themselves useful to the community. The two were often consulted about modern technology and engineering.

The Dalai Lama invited Harrer to be his private tutor. Harrer taught him English, even though Harrer's native language was German. He also taught the 14-year-old boy about the geography, history, and technology of the modern Western world. At their first meeting, Harrer quickly realized how eager the young leader was for this contact. "He beamed all over his face and poured out a flood of questions. He seemed like a person who had for years brooded in solitude over different problems, and now that he had at last someone to talk to, wanted to know all the answers at once."

Harrer was stunned to see that the Dalai Lama had great talent and interest in working with mechanical objects, including music boxes, watches, and mechanical trains. The boy had, on his own, taken apart and pieced back together an old movie projector. The Dalai Lama asked Heinrich Harrer to make a film for him of the ordinary life of his people. That film became the Dalai Lama's introduction to international relations. It led to a friendship with Harrer and to an avenue of learning about and contacting the world outside the Potala.

Harrer and the Dalai Lama installed a generator to power their cinema room, and they regularly showed films. Many of the monk officials disapproved of these activities, but laughed heartily, nonetheless, when they saw themselves on screen. Always animated and enthusiastic when he and Harrer were together, the Dalai Lama was determined not to let the officials prevent their weekly meetings. According to Harrer:

> He was resolved to extend his knowledge beyond purely religious subjects, and it seemed to him that I was the only person who could help him to do so. . . . Like many a good father who wishes to earn the respect of his son, I often spent the evening reviving my knowledge of half-forgotten things or studying new ones. I took the utmost trouble to treat every question seriously and scientifically, as it was clear to me that my answers would form the basis of his knowledge of the Western world.

The Dalai Lama was also fascinated by cars. At that time, there were only four cars in Tibet. They had belonged to the 13th Dalai Lama, so they were at the disposal of the 14th Dalai Lama. He only had to find someone to get them running. He discovered that a man in Lhasa named Tashi Tsering knew about cars, and they worked together until three of the four cars were running.

Even though there were no real roads in Lhasa, the Dalai Lama was determined to try driving. When Tashi Tsering was away and nobody was watching him, the Dalai Lama started a car by turning its ignition crank. He reversed the car out of its garage and drove slowly around the garden at Norbulingka. Suddenly he hit a tree and smashed one of the headlights. Now he had to hide the evidence of his joyride.

Carefully he drove the car back into the garage and then found some glass that he could use to replace the

The Dalai Lama adjusts settings on a motion picture camera.

headlight. The original glass had been tinted, so he coated the new glass with sugar syrup until it looked just like the original. He never knew if Tashi Tsering discovered the damage, but he felt very guilty the next time the two met.

As much as the Dalai Lama loved his games and meetings with Heinrich Harrer, he had less and less free time as he became more involved with his monastic studies and responsibilities. He had to publicly debate many great scholars, and his own nervousness about these challenges kept him studying. He also spent a great deal of time in meditation and in retreat, which helped him develop an inner balance of mind and happiness to support him through difficult times. He wrote:

> For proper development I feel that we need a well-balanced education. We need inner spiritual development to acquire a warm heart which is the basic requirement . . . . A heart full of love and compassion is the main source of inner strength, willpower, happiness, and mental tranquility.

The Dalai Lama was expected to lead many important religious ceremonies. One such ceremony came during *Monlam,* the great springtime prayer festival. At the end of this two-week-long ceremony, the Dalai Lama had to recite a long passage of scripture from memory. Each year he was so nervous about forgetting the words that he had a hard time paying attention to the ceremony itself. "I remember being apoplectic with fear. It dulled my senses to the point where I no longer noticed what was going on around me. . . . When it was over, I was ecstatically happy."

After the Monlam ceremony, which was celebrated throughout the city, the Dalai Lama was allowed to walk through the streets, surrounded by his tutors and attendants. He saw gigantic butter sculptures offered to the

Seated on the lion throne and wearing a gold-peaked cap, the Dalai Lama smiles at his audience.

Buddha, musical and theatrical performances, various competitions, and general gaiety in the city—a great treat for the young leader.

Not all celebrations and processions were strenuous for the Dalai Lama. The summer day each year when he moved from the Potala Palace to Norbulingka gave him the most pleasure. The summer palace was so full of sunlight and flowers that the boy's spirits lifted as soon as the formal procession began. Heinrich Harrer described the spectacular day:

> We heard the blare of trumpets and trombones. The procession approached. The murmurs of the crowd were hushed and a reverent silence reigned, for the head of the column was in sight. A host of serving monks formed the vanguard. With them they carried the God-King's personal effects done up in bundles, each bundle wrapped in a yellow silk cloth. . . . Soon we saw the God-King's favorite birds being carried in their cages . . . behind the servants came monks with banners decorated with texts. Next came a band of mounted musicians wearing brightly colored, old-fashioned garb and playing old-fashioned instruments, from which they produced curious, whimpering sounds.

Harrer went on to describe the parade of dignitaries, household servants, bodyguards, and the commander-in-chief of the army. The people on the sides of the streets stood silently with bowed heads and folded hands. Finally there came the Dalai Lama:

Tibetan horns sound throughout the city on festival days.

Now approached the yellow, silk-lined palanquin of the Living Buddha, gleaming like gold in the sunlight. The bearers were six-and-thirty men in green silk cloaks, wearing red plate-shaped caps. A monk was holding a huge iridescent sunshade made of peacock's feathers over the palanquin. . . . And there he was—bowing to us with a smile behind the glass front of his sedan chair. His finely cut features were full of charm and dignity, but his smile was that of a boy.

During his teenage years, the Dalai Lama steadily carried on his official routines and studies, but he was still too young to participate in the political decision-making of his country. When the Dalai Lama was six, Tathag Rinpoche had taken over the positions of regent and senior tutor. He trained the Dalai Lama for the role of political leader.

Whenever an important political event took place, Tathag Rinpoche decided how much to tell the Dalai Lama. Always curious about political affairs, however, the Dalai Lama found a strategy for spying on the regent. The boy stood on a bureau and peered through a high window in the wall between his room and the regent's. One day in the summer of 1950, the 15-year-old Dalai Lama was looking into the regent's room and witnessed the delivery of a telegram to Tathag Rinpoche.

With a grave look on his face, Tathag Rinpoche read the telegram from the governor of Kham, a province in southeastern Tibet. The governor reported that Chinese Communist soldiers had invaded eastern Tibet. The Chinese claimed that they had come to "liberate Tibet from imperialists"—Westerners living in Tibet. The regent and the Dalai Lama both knew that Tibet could not defend itself against the powerful Chinese People's Liberation Army, the PLA. Tibet had only a small army of 8,500 poorly trained men and very few modern weapons. The regent called together the *kashag,* the Tibetan parliament, for an emergency meeting to discuss ways to hold back the Chinese.

In October 1950, two months after the initial invasion, the PLA sent more than 80,000 soldiers into Tibet on the

Chinese soldiers march into Tibet.

anniversary of the Communist takeover of China. They now planned a full takeover of Tibet.

News of the invasion spread quickly across Tibet, and the people were terrified. They united in prayer and in making public homage to their Buddhist deities. They set out new prayer flags and burned incense—their faith was their only defense. The people lost confidence in their government run by the regent, and they wanted the 15-year-old Dalai Lama to take over the leadership. The people of Lhasa went through the streets hanging posters and singing songs in support of the Dalai Lama. In the past, the Dalai Lama had become the political leader at age 18, but with the grave political situation, the 14th Dalai Lama was installed as political leader on November 17, 1950, at age 15.

The Dalai Lama did not feel prepared to become the political leader. "This filled me with anxiety. . . . I was far from having finished my religious education. I knew nothing about the world and had no experience of politics, and yet I was old enough to know how ignorant I was and how much I still had to learn."

The Dalai Lama was rushed to his political seat, and he faced the crisis of the Communist invasion. He was not fully aware of the intentions of the PLA until his oldest brother, Taktser Rinpoche, came to Lhasa from Kumbum Monastery in the Amdo region. Taktser Rinpoche told his brother the story of the PLA invasion and destruction of Amdo and of his own imprisonment in Kumbum Monastery. In November 1950, the Communists had

> I KNEW NOTHING ABOUT THE WORLD AND HAD NO EXPERIENCE OF POLITICS, AND YET I WAS OLD ENOUGH TO KNOW HOW IGNORANT I WAS AND HOW MUCH I STILL HAD TO LEARN.

taken control of the area and of the monastery. They had held Taktser Rinpoche captive until he pretended to agree to go to Lhasa and persuade the Dalai Lama to allow Communist control of Tibet. The Chinese promised to make him governor of Tibet if he succeeded. They also ordered Taktser Rinpoche to kill the Dalai Lama if the boy resisted.

After telling his story and expressing his opinion that the Communists were untrustworthy and evil, Taktser Rinpoche begged his younger brother to leave Lhasa because there was danger of further invasion. He said that the worst blow to Tibet would be for the Dalai Lama to be placed under Chinese control. Support from powerful foreign governments was Tibet's only hope. Taktser Rinpoche decided to travel to the United States and ask for help.

Now that the Dalai Lama was fully authorized to take political action, he appointed two prime ministers: a monk named Lobsang Tashi and a layperson named Lukhangwa. The two men would rule under him. He then sent out delegations—to the United States, Great Britain, and Nepal—to help Tibet negotiate peace with China. He also sent a delegation to China. On December 20, 1950, the Dalai Lama moved his seat to Yatung, near the Indian border in southern Tibet, to stay out of Chinese hands that were stretching farther and farther into central Tibet.

Trucks transporting Chinese soldiers and supplies move toward the front lines in Tibet.

THE CHINESE TAKEOVER

ALTHOUGH THE DALAI LAMA REMAINED IN YATUNG and was expected to continue his life of study and meditation, he felt a great responsibility for his people. His two prime ministers maintained control of the government in Lhasa and informed him of Chinese movement in Tibet.

After the Chinese had a firm hold of Chamdo, they remained in the eastern region without advancing to central Tibet. They wanted "to assure Tibetans by radio broadcast and pamphlets that they would not alter the traditional social and religious systems." The Chinese maintained, even after destroying Chamdo, that they wanted to carry out a "peaceful liberation" of Tibet from American and British imperialists.

At the same time, Tibetan negotiators were trying hard to rally support in the West and to convince the United Nations to help Tibet defend itself against the Chinese

Communists. The Tibetan delegation sent a long written appeal to the United Nations that described the background of Chinese-Tibetan relations. It gave historical evidence that Tibet was not part of China, as the Chinese claimed, but rather an independent nation that lived peacefully within its mountainous borders—a nation that deserved the right of self-determination.

The United Nations Secretariat ruled that because Tibet was not a member of the United Nations, the appeal would not be treated as an official document. Consequently, members of the United Nations took little action on behalf of the Tibetans. Despite Tibet's friendly relations with Nepal, India, the United States, and Great Britain, these countries did almost nothing to help Tibet. They all feared creating a dispute with China. India stated that it would offer the Dalai Lama a safe encampment inside the Indian border, but India did not want to take arms against the Chinese army. The Tibetans were left feeling isolated and helpless against the powerful Chinese Communists.

Despite his youth, the Dalai Lama understood that part of Tibet's problem was due to its own policy of isolation. For centuries Tibet had maintained laws to keep out foreigners. High-ranking officials did not want any foreign influence interfering with their Buddhist faith. This isolation was easy to keep because of Tibet's location inside forbidding mountain ranges. Foreigners heard only rumors and mythical tales about Tibet. Few outsiders knew anything of Tibetan history, so they believed China's widely publicized reports that claimed Tibet had always been a part of China. But if Tibet had always been a part of the Chinese "Motherland," as the Chinese called it, China would not have to invade Tibet—supposedly part of its own nation—with fully armed troops.

During 1951 the 14th Dalai Lama stayed in Yatung and planned steps to confront the Chinese. The Tibetan people grew uneasy with their government split between Yatung and Lhasa. The nobles began to send women, children, and their wealth to India, in case the Chinese moved into central Tibet.

On May 26, 1951, while the Dalai Lama listened to the Tibetan language broadcast of Radio Peking, he was

At his temporary seat in southern Tibet in 1951, the Dalai Lama is shown a gold urn containing the ashes of two disciples of Buddha who died around 500 B.C.

stunned by news of his delegation in China. The announcer declared that on May 23, Tibet and China had signed a document, the 17-Point Agreement. The announcer said that this agreement "allowed Tibet to come back to the great Chinese Motherland and to reap the benefits of a 'peaceful liberation' by the Chinese." The Chinese claimed Tibet still needed liberation from Western imperialists.

The Dalai Lama was astonished to hear that a document had been signed. He had given his delegation only the power to negotiate, not to make major decisions. He discovered that the Chinese had threatened to use more military force against Tibet if the delegates did not sign the agreement. Wanting to avoid more bloodshed, and believing, as the agreement stated, that the Chinese would not interfere with the existing Tibetan political and religious system, the Tibetan delegates had signed the document. The delegates had not had the official seals of the Dalai Lama's government that would make a document legal and binding for Tibet, so the Chinese had made their own seals for each delegate. Because of this substitution, the 17-Point Agreement was never stamped with the official Tibetan seals that would have indicated the Dalai Lama's approval. Legal experts say that because the Tibetan delegates were coerced into signing the agreement under the threat of a Chinese invasion of Tibet, the 17-Point Agreement "lacked validity under international law."

After signing the agreement, the delegates met with

Mao Tse-tung, chairman of the Chinese Communist Party, who voiced his approval of the negotiations:

> Now you have signed the 17-Point Agreement. That is very good. You have accepted to be part of one big family so now Peking is yours and Shanghai is yours. Now the People's Liberation Army will go to Tibet, do you have any doubts? . . . You will definitely have doubts; it would be very strange if you did not have doubts but there will be a day when your doubts will be cleared away. You will be with the People's Liberation Army so day by day your doubts will be cleared away.

Despite the words of confidence from Mao Tse-tung and the agreement's points stating that China would allow Tibet to preserve its religion, culture, and political system, China claimed a great victory over Tibet. But before the Tibetans knew what was happening, China marched even farther into Tibet and began breaking the 17-Point Agreement.

This was a bleak time for the Dalai Lama. All around him, people were giving him advice and he was not sure whom to trust. His brothers, Thubten Jigme Norbu and Gyalo Thondup, along with many government officials, argued that the Dalai Lama should go into exile in India while the Tibetans continued to seek support from the United States. They urged the Dalai Lama to reject the illegally stamped 17-Point Agreement. On the other hand, many monks in Lhasa wanted the Dalai Lama to return to Lhasa and begin his own negotiations with the Chinese. The monks believed that Tibet would have a better chance of safeguarding its monastic system if it accepted the 17-Point Agreement and maintained negotiations between the Dalai Lama and the Chinese. The monks argued that because Tibet had no patron, no powerful country willing to defend it against China, Tibet must risk that China would not uproot life in Tibet.

The Dalai Lama's brothers worked hard to secure proof that the United States would support Tibet if the Dalai Lama rejected the 17-Point Agreement. Finally, they realized that the United States did not offer any serious hope of preventing the Chinese from taking over Tibet. Even so, "America would serve as a haven where the Dalai Lama could decry Chinese aggression, but from which he could do little to regain his throne. The United States offered to help the Dalai Lama keep alive the flame of Tibetan autonomy and freedom, but little else."

The Dalai Lama felt he had to try to talk directly to Chinese officials. He met with Chinese general Chiang Chin-wu, who tried to convince him that China was truly looking out for Tibet. The general said that China would help Tibet become a modern country like China. This discussion gave the Dalai Lama hope that he would be able to maintain a good compromise with the Chinese. With this optimism, he returned to his seat of power in Lhasa.

When the Dalai Lama reentered Lhasa on August 17, 1951, crowds of Tibetans came out to see him and to celebrate. He was touched to see his welcomers, but he could feel that emotions in the city were tense. People feared that the Chinese would soon reach Lhasa.

General Chiang Chin-wu soon arrived in Lhasa and wasted no time in establishing power. He wanted the Dalai Lama to ratify the 17-Point Agreement. For two months, Tibetans stalled, but finally, in September, the Tibetan National Assembly was called. After lengthy debate, the assembly recommended that the Dalai Lama accept the agreement. The Dalai Lama did so, on October

Chinese military vehicles drive down the streets of Lhasa.

24, 1951, in a telegram to Chairman Mao. He saw no other option for his country.

Soon after, the Chinese general met with the Dalai Lama and the two Tibetan prime ministers, Lobsang Tashi and Lukhangwa, and began to outline reforms. The Dalai Lama tried to keep stable relations with the general, but the prime ministers despised the Chinese official. Chiang Chin-wu refused to deal with anyone other than the Dalai Lama. The Dalai Lama was soon forced, against his personal wishes, to ask his prime ministers to resign.

While the Dalai Lama tried to compromise with the Chinese, the PLA obliterated Tibetan communities in the east. Tension was mounting, and the Dalai Lama realized that the only step he could take was to try again to negotiate with the Communist leaders. In early 1954, he accepted an invitation to visit China, despite his people's fears that China would imprison their leader in Peking.

For about a year, the Dalai Lama and his party— including his family members (except his father, who had died in 1946), his two tutors, the cabinet members, and other Tibetan government officials—toured China. The Chinese wanted to show him the modernizations established by the Communists. A teacher explained Communist theory to him.

The Dalai Lama remained open-minded in his talks with the Chinese. He thought that some Communist principles could work in Tibet, as the country modernized its government. He met with Chairman Mao and was enthusiastic about the possibility of positive cooperation. The

The Dalai Lama and Mao Tse-tung shake hands in Peking.

two got along well, and for a while, the Dalai Lama believed that Mao would deal with Tibet fairly and in good faith. Mao commented on the relationship between Tibet and China: "Tibet is a great country. . . . You have a marvelous history. Long ago you even conquered a lot of China. But now you have fallen behind and we want to help you. In 20 years' time you could be ahead of us and then it will be your turn to help China."

The Dalai Lama accepted Mao's word and held out hope for his country. At the very end of the Dalai Lama's stay in China, however, Mao commented that religion was "poison." After hearing this, the Dalai Lama feared that despite all the negotiations, the Chinese would still try to destroy Tibetan Buddhism.

When the Dalai Lama returned to Tibet in June 1955, he discovered that Mao's words of support had been empty. Chinese forces had gained control throughout Tibet. They helped themselves to Tibet's food storage, food prices escalated, and Tibetans went hungry. Many Tibetan refugees fled from eastern Tibet and flooded Lhasa. With the crowding population came tension and violence. The Chinese still claimed to be helping Tibet.

In the summer of 1956, Chinese troops bombed a large monastery in the eastern Kham region. The Chinese had begun to destroy the religious and cultural artifacts of Tibet. Monasteries were bombed and pillaged. Innocent people were tortured and killed, all for the so-called "liberation" of the Tibetan people. Any Tibetan who resisted the Chinese was considered a traitor and a rebel. Traitors and rebels were murdered.

For the next three years, the conflict grew worse, while the Dalai Lama tried to hold back panic. Without informing the Dalai Lama of the details, his brothers Thubten Jigme Norbu and Gyalo Thondup met with U.S. leaders in hopes of gathering support against the Chinese. Gradually the Tibetans organized secret monetary and military support from the Americans. The U.S. State Department and the CIA agreed to supply arms and begin training Tibetan freedom fighters.

Despite the Tibetan Buddhist belief in nonviolence, the freedom fighters could not let their country fall without a fight. The Chinese forces, however, were too brutal. They crucified, buried alive, beat to death, beheaded, raped, and drowned their Tibetan victims. The Chinese also killed Tibetans by tying them to the backs of galloping horses or skinning them alive.

In Lhasa itself, the Chinese were not openly violent, but they were subtly aggressive. They concealed weapons under their clothing, barricaded themselves in their army camp, and went out only in groups. The Dalai Lama, living in Norbulingka and secluded from city life, was kept informed by his attendants on how Lhasa was changing under Chinese occupation. He soon realized that he might have little time before the country exploded into all-out war, so he decided to finish his monastic duties as soon as possible. He arranged to take his final examinations during the Monlam celebration in March 1959. He would be 23 years old.

During the months before the Dalai Lama's examinations, General Tan Kuan-sen demanded weekly meetings with him. In them the general ordered him to tell the freedom fighters to put down their arms. The Dalai Lama knew that even though he wanted his people to remain nonviolent, he could not expect them to give up easily. He never supported violence, but he could not punish Tibetan patriots.

Chinese troops carve away mountainsides in Tibet to make way for a highway.

Chinese soldiers capture Tibetan monks and confiscate their guns.

During the end of 1958 and the beginning of 1959, the Dalai Lama tried to study Buddhist scripture and practice debate with his tutors. He had difficulty concentrating when he heard daily reports of violence in eastern and central Tibet. The Chinese were said to be building roads and modernizing Tibet, but not for the benefit of the Tibetans. The country seemed full of conspirators, and everyone feared that the Dalai Lama's government would soon be challenged.

The Dalai Lama moved to the Jokhang Temple in central Lhasa, where he would take his final oral exams. On March 1, while the Dalai Lama was making final preparations, he received an invitation to a performance of a

Chinese dance group. The Dalai Lama was too busy to think of entertainment, so he told the Chinese messengers that he would attend the performance when he had finished with his exams. The messengers were annoyed that they could not set a date for the performance.

Meanwhile the city filled up with refugees and pilgrims who had come to worship and celebrate during the Tibetan Monlam ceremony. Thousands of monks came to the Jokhang Temple to witness the Dalai Lama's final debate. From morning to evening, the Dalai Lama answered philosophical questions put to him by other monks. Fortunately, he was well prepared and his examiners judged him worthy of his final *Geyche* degree, similar to a Ph.D. in metaphysics.

Now that he had passed, the Dalai Lama would have to respond to the Chinese invitation. On March 7, after the Dalai Lama returned to Norbulingka, the Chinese officials visited again. Not wanting to insult the Chinese and cause a conflict, the Dalai Lama told them that he would attend the dance performance on March 10. The performance would take place at a theater in the Chinese military camp.

At 6:00 A.M. on March 9, two Chinese officers woke up the *Kusun Depon,* the Dalai Lama's chief bodyguard, and asked him to accompany them to the Chinese camp to make arrangements for the Dalai Lama's visit. The Kusun Depon responded that he would come as soon as he had bathed and eaten breakfast. The two officers grumbled and stomped away, but returned after a short time.

When the Kusun Depon reached the Chinese head-quarters, he found the Chinese general in a bad mood. The general made several demands. He wanted the Dalai Lama to come without his usual retinue of guards, with only a few unarmed attendants. This unusual request caused the Kusun Depon to ask the general why there should not be any bodyguards. The general got angry.

"We don't want any trouble. And the whole thing must be kept secret," demanded the general.

The Kusun Depon returned to Norbulingka and discussed the general's demands with other Tibetan officials. They all became suspicious. The Tibetan people would never allow their leader to go unguarded into the Chinese camp, but the officials did not want to risk upsetting the Chinese. The Dalai Lama decided that he would attend even with the strange conditions. That night neither the Dalai Lama nor his officials slept well.

On the morning of March 10, the Dalai Lama rose with apprehension. After meditation and breakfast, he went outside to walk in his garden. He heard a great noise and asked his attendants to find out what was happening.

They returned to tell him that the palace was surrounded by 30,000 supporters who did not want him to attend the Chinese performance. Somehow they had heard of the Chinese plan and formed a demonstration of protection for their leader. The Dalai Lama asked his officials to call the Chinese and explain that he could not depart through the crowds and that he hoped the crowds would disperse. He sent his regrets.

On March 10, 1959, thousands of Tibetan women surround the Potala Palace in silent protest against the Chinese occupation.

When the Chinese general heard the news, he exploded in anger. "Tibetan reactionaries!" he shouted. "Now we will take drastic measures."

The Dalai Lama tried to calm his people by telling them that he would stay at Norbulingka. Upon hearing this, some Tibetans went home, but the majority refused to move from their spot outside the palace. They continued to demand that Chinese troops be removed from Tibet.

Some people formed groups, denouncing the 17-Point Agreement and shouting their demands. Others moved away from the summer palace, but continued to demonstrate below the Potala Palace and throughout the streets of Lhasa. The Dalai Lama's supporters "were in such a pitch of fury against these unwelcome foreigners with their brutal methods that nothing could move them. They would stay till the end and die keeping guard over their Precious Protector."

The Chinese could not stay calm in all of this chaos. They fortified their troops. The Tibetans thought that the Chinese were preparing for an attack. The Chinese then called the Dalai Lama and suggested that he come to the Chinese camp for his own safety. This was unthinkable, but the Dalai Lama stalled for time by pretending to agree. He asked the Chinese to be patient and wait until the Tibetan demonstrators calmed before the Dalai Lama moved to the Chinese camp.

Day by day, minute by minute, the situation became more unnerving. The Dalai Lama wondered if he should escape now before he was captured by the Chinese. His advisers told him he must leave Tibet because he was the only hope for his people. Finally, on March 17, 1959, the Dalai Lama consulted his divine oracle. With great energy, the oracle told him that he must leave immediately. He gave the Dalai Lama a specific escape route out of the palace and the city. Still unsure, the Dalai Lama went into meditation and did his own divination. The answer was the same. He must escape immediately.

The 23-year-old Dalai Lama waves a bouquet of flowers presented to him upon his arrival in India.

CHAPTER EIGHT

A NEW LIFE
IN EXILE

ON THE COVER OF THE MAY 4, 1959, ISSUE OF *LIFE* magazine is a photograph of the 23-year-old Dalai Lama holding a bouquet of yellow flowers. His smile is deep and wide and he looks joyous.

He had just spent 26 days on horseback and on foot fleeing from war-torn Lhasa to the Indian border. He had been sick with fever and dysentery during the escape. Having learned to overcome personal pain in order to serve humanity, he maintained serenity despite his sadness about the deaths of many of his people. He had done all he could in Lhasa to negotiate for peace with the Chinese. Failing that, he realized that the only way he could help Tibet was to go into exile and tell the world about Tibet's plight.

At the Indian border, a fleet of jeeps met the Dalai Lama's entourage. The Dalai Lama, who had been riding a dzomo during the last leg of his flight, was escorted by

Indian officials to the Indian town of Bomdila. There he received a welcoming telegram from India's prime minister, Pandit Nehru:

> My colleagues and I welcome you and send greetings on your safe arrival in India. We shall be happy to afford the necessary facilities to you, your family and entourage to reside in India. The people of India, who hold you in great veneration, will no doubt accord their traditional respect to your personage. Kind regards to you. Nehru.

After the Dalai Lama recuperated in Bomdila, he and his family traveled to their new home in the Indian town

The Dalai Lama's family includes, from left, *his mother Dekyi Tsering and his siblings, Tsering Dolma, Thubten Jigme Norbu, Gyalo Thondup, Lobsang Samden, the Dalai Lama, Jetsun Pema, and Tenzin Choegyal.*

The Dalai Lama bids farewell to crowds at Tezpur, India.

of Mussoorie. Throughout the journey, international journalists and Indian, Tibetan, and Western friends lined the
streets and shouted their jubilant welcome. One great
cheer was heard above the general roar: *"Dalai Lama Ki
Jai! Dalai Lama Zinda-bad!"* (Hail to the Dalai Lama!
Long live the Dalai Lama!)

The Dalai Lama was moved by this display of respect,
and he was grateful for the help that Nehru had offered.
Nehru, however, was quite guarded about the Dalai
Lama's presence in India. Although Nehru welcomed the
Dalai Lama as a Buddhist leader forced out of his country, he was nervous about offending the Chinese, who
now shared a border with India. He did not want the

Dalai Lama to issue political statements from India because of the likelihood that the Chinese would turn on India for supporting the Dalai Lama.

During his escape from Tibet, the Dalai Lama had issued official statements in order to contradict the lies told by the Chinese. The Chinese claimed that the Dalai Lama had been kidnapped and forced by Western imperialists to reject the 17-Point Agreement. The Dalai Lama issued a statement saying that he had departed on his own free will and that he did, in fact, willingly reject the so-called agreement with China.

In Mussoorie the Dalai Lama dealt with the immediate problem of sheltering thousands of Tibetan refugees who were fleeing from the Chinese. After the Tibetan leader left Norbulingka, the Chinese had bombed the palace and the city. Tibetan reports estimated that at least 100,000 Tibetans died as a result of this attack. Those who survived and could not escape were driven into miserable conditions. Tibetans were starving because the Chinese forced them to give up all of their grain and meat to the Communist soldiers.

Because Chinese Communists did not tolerate religion, they did not allow Tibetans to practice Buddhism. The Communists bombed more than 6,000 Tibetan monasteries and humiliated the Tibetans in an attempt to wipe out Buddhism. They forced Tibetans to kill animals, making them break Buddhist vows against killing. Monks and nuns were made to have sexual relations, which violated their religious convictions.

The Chinese subjected people to "reeducation programs." Tibetans had to attend community lectures in
which the Chinese reiterated the injustice of imperialist
ways and explained the benefits of Chinese Communism.
Tibetans were forced to live by Chinese Communist val-
ues and political ideas, and they began to lose their
cultural identity. If Tibetans objected to Chinese policy in
any way, they were arrested, tortured, and often executed.

In 1959 the PLA sent a memo to Chairman Mao stating
that the Tibetans were not cooperating with the Chinese.

Uniformed Chinese soldiers uphold martial law in Lhasa.

There had been so much opposition to Communist rule that the jails were full of Tibetan reactionaries.

Mao's response to the memo directly contradicted the cooperative attitude he had shown the Dalai Lama in 1954. He said that the feelings of the Tibetans were unimportant; the PLA need not pay attention. The Chinese were not afraid to imprison all Tibetans if necessary. Mao was also informed that the Dalai Lama had escaped Tibet. Mao declared, "In that case, we have lost the battle."

At the same time that the Chinese were imposing such tight restrictions on the Tibetans, they began taking advantage of Tibet's natural resources. They mined Tibet's gold and minerals and cut down forests for timber. They relocated many Han Chinese to Tibet. Their purpose was to ease China's own population explosion and to make Tibetans a minority in their own country.

Refugees who escaped from Tibet risked death by starvation, exposure in the mountains, or disease upon their arrival in the Indian heat and humidity. Miserably sick and worn, many families crossed the border into India with no place to go. With the help of the Indian government, the Dalai Lama set up transit camps for his people. By June 1959, there were 20,000 refugees in India, and more were escaping Tibet every day. Their physical suffering could be relieved a little, but their mental anguish was harder to comfort. One refugee wrote:

> I was overwhelmed with grief that I may never see my country again. It was sad, very sad to lose one's family, but I felt anger and pain when I realized that

Tibet was being brutally attacked by the Chinese. The
cunning cat had caught the mice. We may never have
our own country. What will happen to our people
and our beloved leader His Holiness the Dalai Lama?
One felt so lost, so helpless and powerless.

In the two main Indian transit camps, life was
ghastly—with poor sanitation and shelter—but it was better than living under Communist occupation. Tibetans
were accustomed to living in the cold, dry air of a high
altitude, and they had difficulty adapting to the heat and
humidity at the camps. Many died from heat stroke and
tuberculosis.

As soon as he learned the details of the refugee situation, the Dalai Lama asked the Indian government to
relocate the Tibetans to a more suitable area. After some
negotiating, Nehru found a way to move the Tibetans to
northern India, where Tibetans could live at a higher
elevation, and employed many of them in road construction. He helped the Dalai Lama set up a Tibetan school
system to educate the children and to preserve the threatened Tibetan culture. The Dalai Lama credits India for
its generosity:

Over the years now, the people and Government
of India have given an extraordinary amount to us
Tibetan refugees . . . despite their own enormous economic difficulties. I doubt whether any other refugees have been so well treated by their hosts. . . . Yet
in a way, it is only right that India should come to our
aid. For Buddhism came to Tibet from India, along

with many other important cultural influences. There is no doubt in my mind that she has a better claim on Tibet than China, whose influence was only ever slight. I often compare the relationship between India and Tibet with that between a teacher and a pupil. When the pupil gets him or herself into difficulty, it is the responsibility of the teacher to come to the pupil's assistance.

The Dalai Lama met with the many journalists who had been waiting months for a formal statement from him. The young leader formally rejected as invalid the 17-Point Agreement a second time. He explained that because China had never observed the agreement forced upon the Tibetan negotiators, Tibet now saw no legal obligation to accept the terms. The Dalai Lama also declared official his Tibetan government in exile. With the Dalai Lama's announcement, the Indian government bristled again. Fear of China compelled the Indian government to issue a statement that it would not recognize the Dalai Lama's government.

Early in his exile, the Dalai Lama took great steps to modernize Tibet's governmental system. After setting up a government in exile, he drafted a constitution to prepare Tibetans for political independence when they regained their country. He organized a body of people's representatives from each of Tibet's three provinces, and he encouraged women to take on governmental responsibility. His siblings helped him a great deal by continuing negotiations with foreign governments, supervising

The Dalai Lama set up schools for Tibetan refugees in Dharamsala.

refugee camps, and organizing hospitals, orphanages, and schools. The Dalai Lama promoted the continuation of Tibetan arts through the creation of the Tibetan Institute of Performing Arts, which produced traditional Tibetan operas and taught Tibetan music and drama to students.

The Dalai Lama made himself available to all people and removed the great ceremony that had traditionally

distanced him from others. Although in the past he had
sat on a platform that had raised him above others, he
now insisted that his guests sit on a chair the same level
as his. He granted audiences to people of all levels of society. Some of his officials disagreed with these changes,
but the Dalai Lama realized that Tibet should not return
to a feudal system in which the wealthy and powerful
people oppressed the poor, nor should the Dalai Lama be
seen as almighty and distant from the rest of the world.
Tibet needed the world's help.

*Pandit Nehru and his daughter, Indira Gandhi, meet with the Dalai
Lama in September 1959.*

After only a short time in exile, the Dalai Lama became successful at public relations. Upon meeting the Dalai Lama, journalists and other visitors were surprised at how natural and friendly he was. He knew how to make a guest feel comfortable. Foreigners often wondered if they should prostrate themselves on the floor as the Tibetans did when meeting the Dalai Lama. Realizing immediately his guests' discomfort, the Dalai Lama was quick to smile, extend his hand for a handshake, and lead them to a seat close by him. He was as attentive as an affectionate uncle. He listened carefully, patted his guest on the hand, and laughed wholeheartedly at the slightest hint of humor.

During the end of 1959 and the beginning of 1960, the Dalai Lama spent much of his time meeting with Nehru, talking with foreign heads of state, and trying to arrange a hearing on Tibet in the United Nations. After intense negotiations, the Federation of Malaya and the Republic of Ireland sponsored a draft resolution about Tibet, which was debated in the United Nations general assembly. Foreign committees offered aid to Tibet, but even with this support, the Dalai Lama knew that he had to look at his exile as long-term. He had to help Tibetans plan a reorganization and self-governing system for their life in exile and their eventual return to Tibet.

In 1960 the Indian government moved the Dalai Lama, his family, and his entourage to another mountain town, Dharamsala, a 12-hour drive north of Delhi. At first, the Dalai Lama suspected that this move was a way for the Indian government to keep the Tibetans hidden from

The Dalai Lama's monastery in Dharamsala

public attention. But Tibetan officials inspected the village and reported that Dharamsala had a mountainous climate similar to Tibet. It would be a good place for the Tibetans to live.

In the spring of 1960, the Dalai Lama moved his political and religious offices to Dharamsala. He also accepted a gift of 3,000 acres of land in southern India for newly forming Tibetan refugee communities.

On March 10, 1960, marking the first anniversary of the Tibetan people's uprising, the Dalai Lama made an important speech to his people and to the world. He told his people not to hope for an immediate return to Tibet, but to help themselves by rebuilding their society and by preserving their culture. "As to the future, I stated my belief that, with Truth, Justice, and Courage as our weapons, we Tibetans would eventually prevail in regaining freedom for Tibet." Thus began his yearly tradition of a March 10 announcement.

The Dalai Lama addresses his followers in a ceremony celebrating the anniversary of the Tibetan uprising against the Chinese Communists.

The Dalai Lama at home in Dharamsala

CHAPTER NINE

LIVING FOR PEACE

FROM A SECLUDED LIFE IN A DARK PALACE HIGH above Lhasa to a busy life of near-constant travel and daily interviews, the Dalai Lama has not been unhappy to adapt his lifestyle. He is only sad that he could not do so in his own country.

Since 1960 the Dalai Lama has kept an active schedule of daily spiritual practice in his modest home in Dharamsala, India, followed by political activities in his office and meetings in his audience room, which is adorned with little more than a green rug, a green couch, a coffee table, and a wide green chair. The Dalai Lama usually sits on the wide chair when listening to his guests or his cabinet ministers.

Each morning he wakes up at 4:00 A.M. He recites mantras, words that help still the mind. Then he drinks a cup of hot water and takes Tibetan herbal medicine, which he says helps him stay healthy. Next he makes numerous prostrations on the floor, showing respect to the Buddhas. Then he bathes and goes outside for a walk—all of this before his 5:15 breakfast, during which he reads Buddhist scripture.

After breakfast the Dalai Lama meditates for two hours—interrupting meditation to listen to a short British radio news program—and then studies Buddhist philosophy for four hours. For a brief time before lunch, he reads official correspondence or the newspaper, and then he reads scripture again during his lunch, usually his final meal of the day.

Sometimes the Dalai Lama writes during the morning. He is the author of more than 20 books on Buddhist philosophy and on the general human condition. These books have been distributed throughout the world, bringing the Dalai Lama's compassionate words to people of all races, religions, and social backgrounds. His ideas have won him a great deal of attention, which he seeks not for himself but for his countrymen and women. A steady stream of visitors journey to the Tibetan community in Dharamsala.

After all of his morning activity, he gives audiences to people who want to talk to him about politics, Buddhist practice, humanitarian projects, or his personal beliefs. He talks to guest after guest until about 5:00 in the evening, when he relaxes before having tea. Finally, after tea he says prayers until his 9:00 P.M. bedtime.

On special days, he alters his schedule to give a teaching to the public. On these days, masses of Tibetans,

Indians, and foreign visitors come up the paved driveway to Namgyal Monastery next to the Dalai Lama's residence. There they circle the main temple in customary clockwise fashion and offer prostrations in front of the main entrance, where they can see the Dalai Lama on his red and gold throne. Then the people assemble on the ground and listen to the Dalai Lama's teaching. If he gives blessings after his talk, each worshiper approaches him, offers him a sacred white scarf called a *kata,* then receives a red silk cord signifying his blessing.

A group of pilgrims, holding katas *around their necks, wait to meet the Dalai Lama.*

Even when the Dalai Lama travels, he tries to do at least five hours of meditation and study each day. Since 1967 he has been invited to more than 40 countries in Asia, Europe, and North and South America. He has given Buddhist teachings at Tibetan centers throughout the world, met dignitaries in his effort to seek political attention for Tibet, spoken out about universal responsibility and spiritual awareness, and received awards for his promotion of peace and goodwill.

The Dalai Lama greets Prince Charles of England during one of his many trips abroad.

In 1989 the Dalai Lama won the Nobel Prize for Peace because of his continued efforts to make peace with China. He has proposed several peace plans, including the Five Point Peace Plan, in which he suggested transforming Tibet into a zone of peace and eliminating all nuclear weapon manufacturing and waste disposal. The Chinese response to these proposals has always been negative.

For over 30 years, the Dalai Lama has never advocated violence against China, even though Tibetan fact-finding missions have reported that the Chinese still violate Tibetans' human rights and destroy Tibet's environment through deforestation and nuclear waste dumping. He has always said that violence only begets more violence, and therefore the path of violence will never lead to freedom or happiness. In his acceptance speech for the Nobel prize, he humbly thanked the Nobel committee and reiterated his belief in nonviolence:

"I am no one special," said the Dalai Lama. "But I believe the prize is a recognition of the true value of altruism, love, compassion, and nonviolence which I try to practice, in accordance with the teachings of the Buddha and the great sages of India and Tibet."

For the Dalai Lama, spiritual practice—praying and meditating—is the base of his life. "To engender altruism, or compassion, in myself, I practice certain mental exercises which promote love towards all sentient beings, including my so-called enemies."

The Dalai Lama sees no conflict in being involved in

both politics and religion. Indeed, he believes that any deed done with good motivation is a religious act. Good motivation makes a person spiritual. He believes that because politicians are responsible for so many people, they must have an active moral life.

> Politicians need religion even more than a hermit on retreat. If a hermit acts out of bad motivation, he harms no one but himself. But if someone who can directly influence the whole of society acts with bad motivation, then a great number of people will be adversely affected.

As a leader, the Dalai Lama influences Tibetans —both those in exile and those in Tibet—and the world. His ideas and actions know no political boundaries. His main goal is to end the abuse of human rights in Tibet, but no less important is his work to promote world peace. He often tells listeners that through their individual efforts, they can contribute to universal happiness:

> I believe that the purpose of life is to be happy. From the moment of birth, every human being wants happiness and does not want suffering. From the very core of our being, we simply desire contentment. I don't know whether the universe, with its countless galaxies, stars and planets, has a deeper meaning or not, but at the very least, it is clear that we humans who live on this earth face the task of making a happy life for ourselves. Therefore, it is important to discover what will bring about the greatest degree of happiness.

He believes that when we discover a true source of happiness, we often want to share that with others. If we can remember that other people also want happiness and are trying to avoid suffering, then we become stronger by trying to ease the suffering of all beings.

> Thus we can strive gradually to become more compassionate, that is we can develop both genuine sympathy for others' suffering and the will to help remove their pain. As a result, our own serenity and inner strength will increase.

THUS WE CAN STRIVE GRADUALLY TO BECOME MORE COMPASSIONATE, THAT IS WE CAN DEVELOP BOTH GENUINE SYMPATHY FOR OTHERS' SUFFERING AND THE WILL TO HELP REMOVE THEIR PAIN.

Having compassion for all beings on this planet and being universally responsible are two of the most essential philosophies of the Dalai Lama.

The Dalai Lama's energy for helping others seems endless, and despite all of his political responsibilities, he never neglects his spiritual practice that helps him maintain his personal calmness and goodwill:

> I feel that the Buddhist emphasis on love and patience has helped us considerably in coming through this difficult period of our history. It has helped us maintain a sense of clarity, strength, and humor. Although almost a quarter of our population was killed by the Red Guard, the Tibetan people can still smile and laugh. They can still look to the future with eyes of hope. We call it *sem-yangpo*, the good heart.

The Dalai Lama believes the invasion of his country was prophesied, as was the spread of Tibetan Buddhism to the West and the eventual re-gaining of the Tibetan homeland. With great patience, he prepares his people in exile for a new life, if and when Tibetans are suc-cessful in negotiations with the Chinese. Tibetan communities in exile have been established in many parts of the world—India, Nepal, Bhutan, Europe, Canada, and the United States. Tibetan refugees are bound together by their strong spiritual practice, their common interest to save Tibet, and their love of the Dalai Lama. One young Tibetan in Dharamsala wrote about Tibetans' respect for their exiled leader:

> ALTHOUGH ALMOST A QUARTER OF OUR POPULATION WAS KILLED BY THE RED GUARD, THE TIBETAN PEOPLE CAN STILL SMILE AND LAUGH. THEY CAN STILL LOOK TO THE FUTURE WITH EYES OF HOPE.

> Currently, we live under the impending danger of mindless Chinese sweeping Tibetans out of Tibet with their sinister policy of population trans-fer. . . . The situation is indeed grim.
>
> But the silver lining on the dark cloud of our sit-uation is the presence of a unique leadership in the person of His Holiness the Dalai Lama, "an incurable optimist" as someone has described him.

During the 1970s, the Chinese indicated that they were interested in negotiations with the Tibetan government in exile. The Chinese allowed the Dalai Lama to send sev-eral fact-finding delegations to Tibet to assess life under Chinese occupation. When the delegations arrived, they were mobbed by Tibetans who wanted to know about the Dalai Lama. Despite public orders from the Chinese government to stay away from the delegations, the Tibetan people crushed into the streets to touch the exiled Tibetans and ask for pictures of the Dalai Lama. The Chinese have claimed that Tibetans are happier under Chinese rule and that they do not want to be led by the Dalai Lama, but this claim is easily proven false.

Since the 1980s, tourists to Tibet have reported that Tibetans everywhere beg for pictures of the exiled Dalai Lama. Tibetans ask the tourists to tell the rest of the world that Tibetans want an end to Chinese oppression and that they still honor the Dalai Lama. When such stories reach the West, the Chinese are embarrassed and angered.

Tibetans have often staged peaceful demonstrations for independence. The Chinese have responded with violence. According to monks who recently escaped Tibet and foreign tourists who witnessed the demonstrations, the Chinese have fired directly upon the demonstrators, killing many of them. The Chinese still regularly torture and imprison Tibetan demonstrators and their family members.

After a demonstration in October 1987, the Chinese government imposed a curfew on Lhasa, ordered all tourists and journalists out of Tibet, and arrested anyone suspected of proindependence activities. In January 1988, the Associated Press reported that more than 5,000 Tibetans—adults and children—were imprisoned and

Tibetan demonstrators march through the streets of Lhasa. After three days of proindependence rioting, China declared martial law in Lhasa.

tortured: blinded, maimed, hung, and stabbed in the mouth, eyes, and genitals with electric cattle prods.

The Dalai Lama was not surprised by the reports of violence. The Chinese had not changed their overall policy and actions since 1950. He has difficulty trusting the Chinese leaders, who have lied again and again about the situation inside Tibet. According to the Dalai Lama, some good has come from the more recent tragic events in Tibet—the world has been made aware of the Tibetan situation. Major television networks and newspapers have frequently reported the violations against human rights in Tibet, causing the general public and foreign governments to take action against the Chinese government.

Newly formed Tibetan support groups in the West have created newsletters and computer networks to spread the word about the Tibetan situation. Although the Chinese still deny reports of violence inside Tibet and refuse to respond to the Dalai Lama's new proposals to negotiate for the future of Tibet, the world is now paying attention to the Land of Snows.

In 1991, during a speech at Yale University, the Dalai Lama announced that he was considering going to Tibet to assess the situation himself and to remind his people not to abandon nonviolent methods for peace. "My visit could have provided a new opportunity to promote understanding and create a basis for a negotiated solution to the issue of Tibet," said the Dalai Lama in private correspondence. "Unfortunately, the Chinese government's reaction to my proposal has been negative."

In the 1990s, the Dalai Lama intensified the democratization process by making important policy changes in the Tibetan government in exile. He began drafting the future democratic constitution for Tibet, which states that the Dalai Lama will no longer be head of the political system. Tibetans will elect a leader.

Many Tibetans are saddened that their beloved leader wishes to remove himself from politics, but the Dalai Lama believes that the monastic system must be replaced by a democratic system that suits Tibet. His primary goal is to do what is best for his people. In the future, the Dalai Lama hopes to be able to act only as a private citizen and a "simple Buddhist monk."

As for his reincarnation, the Tibetan leader says that the institution of the Dalai Lama is dependent upon the needs and wishes of all Tibetans. Should his people choose a reincarnation by the old method, then his reincarnation

The Dalai Lama smiles at his audience before the "Festival of Tibet 2000" program in Bombay, India. He gave a speech on "Ethics for the New Millennium."

would appear in a free country. He wouldn't appear in Tibet, where he would be controlled by the Chinese government. The purpose of his reincarnation is to complete the unfinished tasks of the previous Dalai Lama.

In 1999, the Dalai Lama expressed his hopes for China and Tibet, saying that the future would bring friendship, respect, and cooperation between the two countries.

The Dalai Lama has continually been a forward-thinking individual who acts with compassion for all beings. In private and in public, he never sways from his commitment to remove suffering whenever and wherever he can.

> I believe that to meet the challenge of our times, human beings will have to develop a greater sense of universal responsibility. Each of us must learn to work not just for his or her own self, family, or nation, but for the benefit of all humankind. Universal responsibility is the real key to human survival. It is the best foundation for world peace.

SOURCES

11 Dalai Lama XIV (Bstan-'dzin-rgya-mtsho), *Buddhism in Practice* (New York: Potala), 4.

13–14 Dalai Lama XIV, *Freedom in Exile: An Autobiography of the Dalai Lama* (New York: HarperCollins, 1990), 136.

14 Ibid., 138.

18 Dalai Lama XIV, interview by author, Dharamsala, India, 6 October 1987.

19 Dalai Lama XIV, *Freedom in Exile,* 8.

21 Ibid., 9.

21 Ibid.

29 Ibid., 33–34.

29 Charles Bell, *Portrait of the Dalai Lama* (London: Wisdom, 1987), 355–356.

34 Sonam Wangdu, *The Discovery of the XIVth Dalai Lama* (Bangkok: Klett Thai, 1975), 12.

35 Ibid., 15.

38 Ibid., 25.

38 Ibid.

40 Ibid., 29.

40 Ibid.

43 Dalai Lama XIV, *Freedom in Exile,* 13.

44 Ibid., 14.

48–49 Roger Hicks & Ngakpa Chogyam, *Great Ocean* (Great Britain: Element, 1984), 61.

49 Dalai Lama XIV, *Freedom in Exile,* 20.

52 Ibid., 24.

55 Ibid., 19.

55 Dalai Lama XIV, *Ocean of Wisdom: Guidelines for Living* (San Francisco: Harper and Row, 1990), 30.

56 Dalai Lama XIV, *Freedom in Exile,* 22.

57–58 Ibid., 25.

62 Melvyn C. Goldstein, *A History of Modern Tibet, 1913–1951* (Berkeley: University of California State, 1989), 5.

64 Vijay Kranti, *Dalai Lama Speaks* (New Delhi: Centrasia, 1990), 101.

65 Heinrich Harrer, *Seven Years in Tibet* (Los Angeles: J. P. Tarcher, 1981), 273.

66 Ibid., 273–275.

68 Kranti, *Dalai Lama Speaks,* 109.

68–69 Dalai Lama XIV, *Freedom in Exile,* 41.

70 Harrer, *Seven Years in Tibet,* 187–188.

71 Ibid., 186–189.

74 Dalai Lama XIV, *My Land and My People* (New York: Potala, 1983), 83.

77 Goldstein, *A History of Modern Tibet,* 740.

80 Radio Peking, 26 May 1951.

80 *The Legal Status of Tibet* (Dharamsala: Office of Information and International Relations, 1989), ix.

81 Goldstein, *A History of Modern Tibet,* 770–771.

82 Ibid., 803.

85 Dalai Lama XIV, *Freedom in Exile,* 89.

91 The former Kusung Depon, interview by author, Dharamsala, India, 27 July 1988.

92 Ibid.

93 Dalai Lama XIV, *Freedom in Exile,* 135.

96 Ibid., 144.

97 Ibid., 145.

100 Ibid., 221.

100–101 Namgyal Lhamo Taklha, "Endless Rise of Mountains."

101–102 Dalai Lama XIV, *Freedom in Exile,* 150.

107 Ibid., 159.

113 Dalai Lama XIV, "Acceptance Speech by His Holiness, the Dalai Lama of Tibet, University Aula, Oslo, Dec. 10, 1989," in *Nobel Prize for Peace: Collected Speeches,* (Dharamsala: The Tibetan Office of Information and International Relations, 1990), 15.

113 Dalai Lama XIV, *Freedom in Exile,* 207.

114 Ibid., 202–203.

114 Dalai Lama XIV, *Compassion and the Individual* (Boston: Wisdom, 1991), 3.

115 Ibid., 3–4.

115 Glenn H. Mullin, *A Long Look Homeward: An Interview with the Dalai Lama of Tibet* (New York: Snow Lion, Potala, and the Tibetan Cultural Center, 1987), 29.

116 Lobsang Yeshi, letter to author, December 1992.

119 Dalai Lama XIV, letter to author, 17 April 1992.

121 Dalai Lama XIV, "Universal Responsibility and Our Global Environment" (speech presented at the Global Forum, Rio de Janeiro, Brazil, June 7, 1992).

P H O T O   A C K N O W L E D G E M E N T S

Photographs are used with permission of: Jules Hermes, pp. 2 (both), 6, 11, 106, 111, 122; map by John Erste, p. 8; Tibetan Office of Information, Dharamsala, pp. 12, 57; AP/Wide World Photos, pp. 15, 83, 85, 88, 89, 94, 120; © Bettmann/Corbis, pp. 16, 25, 37, 42, 43, 46, 53, 67, 73, 76, 79, 99, 107, 118; Connie Bickman, pp. 18, 19; Sidney Piburn, Snow Lion Publications, Inc., p. 22; Stephen Batchelor, p. 26; The Newark Museum, pp. 28, 45, 59; Mr. George Tsarong, pp. 32, 62; Archive Photos, pp. 50, 60, 69, 71, 92, 97, 104, 108; Whitney Stewart, pp. 63, 103, 128; Thubten Norbu, p. 96; © Clive Arrowsmith/Camarapress/Retna Ltd., p. 112.

Front cover: © C. Geral/Retna Ltd.
Back cover: © Linus Morgan/Retna Ltd.

B I B L I O G R A P H Y

Selected Writings of the 14th Dalai Lama

The Art of Happiness: A Handbook for Living. With Howard C. Cutler. New York: Putnam, 1998.

The Bodhgaya Interviews. Edited by Jose Ignacio Cabezon. New York: Snow Lion, 1988.

Ethics for the New Millenium. New York: Riverhead Books, 1999.

Freedom in Exile: An Autobiography of the Dalai Lama. New York: HarperCollins, 1990.

A Human Approach to World Peace. London: Wisdom, 1984.

Path to Bliss: A Practical Guide to Stages of Meditation. Translated by Geyshe Thubten Jinpa. Edited by Christine Cox. New York: Snow Lion, 1991.

Spiritual Advice for Buddhists and Christians. Edited by Donald W. Mitchell. New York: Continuum, 1998.

Tibet, China and the World: A Compilation of Interviews. Dharamsala: Narthang, 1989.

The Way to Freedom. San Francisco: HarperSanFrancisco, 1994.

Other Sources

Avedon, John. *In Exile from the Land of Snows.* London: Michael Joseph, 1984.

Bell, Charles. *Portrait of a Dalai Lama: The Life and Times of the Great Thirteenth.* 1946. London: Wisdom, 1987.

Dundul Namgyal Tsarong. *What Tibet Was.* New Delhi: Pradeep Malhotra, 1990.

Gibb, Christopher. *A History of Tibet.* Book 1, *The Land of the Snows.* Dharamsala: Tibetan Children's Village, 1984.

———. *A History of Tibet.* Book 2, *Independence to Exile.* Dharamsala: Tibetan Children's Village, 1987.

Goldstein, Melvyn C. *A History of Modern Tibet, 1913–1951.* Berkeley: University of California State, 1989.

Harrer, Heinrich. *Seven Years in Tibet. 1953.* Los Angeles: J. P. Tarcher, 1981.

Hicks, Roger & Ngakpa Chogyam. *Great Ocean.* Great Britain: Element, 1984.

Kranti, Vijay. *Dalai Lama Speaks.* New Delhi: Centrasia, 1990.

Malik, I. L. *Dalai Lamas of Tibet: Succession of Births.* New Delhi: Uppal, 1984.

Mitter, J. P. *Betrayal of Tibet.* New Delhi: Allied, 1964.

Mullin, Glenn H. *A Long Look Homeward: An Interview with the Dalai Lama of Tibet.* New York: Snow Lion, Potala, and the Tibetan Cultural Center, 1987.

Namgyal Lhamo Taklha. "Endless Rise of Mountains." 1993.

Sonam Wangdu. *The Discovery of the XIVth Dalai Lama.* Bangkok: Klett Thai, 1975.

Thubten Jigme Norbu and Heinrich Harrer. *Tibet Is My Country.* London: Wisdom, 1986.

Tsepon W. D. Shakabpa. *Tibet: A Political History.* New Haven: Yale University Press, 1967.

A B O U T   T H E   A U T H O R

Whitney Stewart writes fiction and nonfiction, with a special interest in life in the Himalayan mountains. She has traveled to Tibet, Nepal, and Dharamsala, India where she lived with a Tibetan family. She has also written a biography of Sir Edmund Hillary for Lerner Publications.

Other paperback editions in the Biography® series:

BILL GATES	LEGENDS OF DRACULA
BRUCE LEE	MARK TWAIN
GEORGE LUCAS	MUHAMMAD ALI
JESSE VENTURA	PRINCESS DIANA
JIMI HENDRIX	ROSIE O'DONNELL
JOHN GLENN	STEVEN SPIELBERG
LATIN SENSATIONS	WOMEN OF THE WILD WEST